Praise for the previous edition of
Getting Your Child Back to School

"The information and strategies presented in this book are rich in providing parents with answers to many of their 'why' and 'how' questions. Parents will come away understanding the nature of their child's school refusal problem, the factors contributing to the problem, and effective strategies for returning their child to school in a positive and productive manner."—**Anne Marie Albano**, PhD, ABPP, Director, Columbia University Clinic for Anxiety and Related Disorders

"Using his research background as well as his years of clinical experience, Dr. Kearney describes the variety of reasons that drive school refusal behavior in youth and then provides clear and effective solutions for each type of problem. Parents struggling mightily to get their child to go to and stay in school will welcome Dr. Kearney's sage advice."—**Patricia M. DiBartolo**, PhD, Caroline L. Wall '27 Professor of Psychology, Smith College

"Written by one of the leading experts in this area, this book is a must-read for parents of children who are reluctant or refuse to attend school."—**Cynthia G. Last**, PhD, Author of *Help for Worried Kids*

T0303135

Getting Your Child Back to School

A Parent's Guide to Solving School Attendance Problems, Revised and Updated Edition

Christopher A. Kearney

OXFORD
UNIVERSITY PRESS

OXFORD
UNIVERSITY PRESS

Oxford University Press is a department of the University of Oxford. It furthers the University's objective of excellence in research, scholarship, and education by publishing worldwide. Oxford is a registered trade mark of Oxford University Press in the UK and certain other countries.

Published in the United States of America by Oxford University Press
198 Madison Avenue, New York, NY 10016, United States of America.

Library of Congress Cataloging-in-Publication Data
Names: Kearney, Christopher A., author.
Title: Getting your child back to school : a parent's guide to solving school attendance problems, Revised and Updated Edition / Christopher A. Kearney.
Other titles: Getting your child to say "yes" to school
Description: Revised and updated edition. | New York, NY :
Oxford University Press, 2021. | Revised edition of: Getting your child to say "yes" to school. 2007 |
Includes bibliographical references and index. |
Identifiers: LCCN 2020047324 (print) | LCCN 2020047325 (ebook) |
ISBN 9780197547496 (paperback) | ISBN 9780197547519 (epub) |
ISBN 9780197547526 (Digital-Online)
Subjects: LCSH: School phobia.
Classification: LCC RJ506.S33 K418 2021 (print) |
LCC RJ506.S33 (ebook) | DDC 618.92/8522—dc23
LC record available at https://lccn.loc.gov/2020047324
LC ebook record available at https://lccn.loc.gov/2020047325

DOI: 10.1093/med-psych/9780197547496.001.0001

1 3 5 7 9 8 6 4 2

Printed by LSC Communications, United States of America

Contents

Foreword

School attendance problems continue to be a serious challenge for parents and youth, especially in this day and age. Many kids are faced with intense academic and social challenges, systemic barriers to school attendance and graduation, and overcrowded and underfunded schools. In addition, at this writing, a pandemic continues to sweep the globe and cause massive disruptions to the educational process. Many kids have been forced to learn at home or engage in online learning or a hybrid approach that can be disjointed and unsettling. Extended absences from school, whether forced or not, can cause substantial distress and disruption to youth and their families. This new edition is a parent guide to solving common school attendance problems and challenges in different times. The edition covers not only school attendance problems during "normal" times but also suggestions as well for coping with challenges during extended periods of time when school is closed.

1

What Are School Attendance Problems?

"Jonathan has missed the last week of school! I can't seem to get him out of bed in the morning. I feel so frustrated. What can I do?"

"Ashlee has a lot of trouble going to school in the morning. She cries a lot and seems so unhappy. This is so stressful for all of us. How can we help our daughter?"

"I just found out that Reggie has been skipping some classes at school. I can't believe it! Why is he doing this? What happens now?"

"Will just seems to mope around, especially on Sunday nights. He's always asking us to let him stay home. I'm so confused. Should I let him stay home for a few days?"

"I can get Madison to go to school but only after a long argument every morning! I'm so tired of this. What can we do to make the morning easier?"

"Valentina cries all the time at school and always wants me there. She hangs on to me at the playground as I try to drop her off. I feel so bad for her. Should I miss a few days of work and go to class with her?"

"Brett always seems to have stomachaches and headaches in the morning before school. He says he can't go. Should I make him go? What's wrong?"

Do any of these situations sound familiar to you? When a child has trouble attending school, or seems so unhappy about going to school, family members are often frustrated, distressed, shocked, confused, and angry. But that's understandable. We naturally expect our children to eat their dinner, play with friends, sleep at night—and go to school in the morning! If a child has trouble doing any of these things, then family tension builds, everyone argues, and you may start wondering: What do we do now? What is going to happen? How can I get my child back to school? All of these reactions are normal.

Having a child with trouble attending school is upsetting because we do not like for our kids to be distressed, and we worry what will happen if they don't receive their education. And, let's face it, we have work and other things to do! I know the rush in the morning and what can happen if a child does not want to leave the home. What makes trouble attending school even more upsetting is that the problem can be hard to understand and resolve. But be assured: You *can* get your child to school with less distress! The main purpose of this book is to cover the different aspects of this problem and give you the means to handle all kinds of school attendance problems.

Types of School Attendance Problems

School attendance problems refer to any difficulty attending school or remaining in classes for an entire day. Other terms, such as truancy or chronic absenteeism, are sometimes used when discussing attendance problems, but these terms are often defined differently depending on a certain area. I use the term "school attendance problems" because it includes *all* children who have trouble going to or being in school. In other words, your child's situation should be in this book!

A child may have different *kinds* of school attendance problems. A brief look at these problems is provided in Figure 1.1. A longer look at these problems follows here. Think about the problems that seem to apply most to your child and place a check mark next to those that do.

X- - - - - - - - - - X- - - - - - - - - X- - - - - - - X- - - - - - - - - X- - - - - - - - - X- - - - - - - - - X- - - - - - - - - X

School attendance with stress and pleas for nonattendance	Repeated misbehaviors in the morning to avoid school	Repeated tardiness in the morning followed by attendance	Periodic absences or skipping of classes	Repeated absences or skipping of classes mixed with attendance	Complete absence from school during a certain period of time	Complete absence from school for an extended period of time

Figure 1.1 Forms of school attendance problems.

- Camila does in fact go to school but is often stressed while there and cries or has stomachaches or headaches when near school. She always seems to be pestering her mom and dad to stay home and constantly asks for home-based instruction. Camila also clings to her parents in the morning as they try to get her into the school building.
- Hunter hopes to miss school by misbehaving in the morning; his common behaviors include dawdling, refusing to move, locking himself in a room or car, and having temper tantrums. Hunter's parents often get their son to school but only after a huge battle between 6 a.m. and 9 a.m.
- Stacy is often late to school as a result of dawdling or the other misbehaviors just mentioned for Hunter. She often shows up to school during a second-period class or at 10:30 that morning. Sometimes she is very anxious in the morning as well.
- Parker will attend school only if one of his parents stays with him at school.
- Jackson skips one or more classes during the day, such as ditching school after lunch to be with friends or missing a class that requires a test or oral presentation that day. He also has trouble eating in the school cafeteria with others.
- Melissa misses a complete school day about once or twice per week.
- Garrett has a history of missing long stretches of school days, such as a couple of weeks or even an entire semester.

Which of these situations sounds most familiar to you? Does your child have an attendance problem that is different from the ones listed here? If so, describe it by writing in this space:

_____

_____

_____

_____

Did you place several check marks next to the attendance problems I listed? If you did, that's okay. Many children with trouble attending school show different kinds of attendance problems. Consider the case of Justin:

> Justin is a 12-year-old boy who has just entered middle school and is having problems adjusting to the new setting. He seems a bit overwhelmed by the fact that he suddenly has several new teachers and classes and much more homework than before. In addition, Justin is nervous about so many of the older kids at his school and whether he will miss the bus after school. Lately he has been having problems getting up in the morning. During the past week alone, Justin refused to leave home on Monday in an attempt to miss school, skipped a class at school on Tuesday, was completely absent from school on Wednesday, was late to school on Thursday, and had no trouble attending school on Friday!

Obviously, a situation like Justin's can be frustrating for everyone involved. A main challenge of school attendance problems is their *unpredictability*: A parent is often unsure what kind of problems to expect on any given morning. This is why a key goal of this book is to cover *all* of the attendance problems you are likely to see in the morning and during the school day and to help you address each of these. Let's talk more about what this book is about.

What Is This Book About?

The main purpose of this book is to help parents and kids find solutions to school attendance problems. In doing so, I am relying on many years of experience working with these groups and helping parents get their kids back to school. As such, I can provide *very specific suggestions* for what you can do in the morning and the rest of the day to ensure that your child goes to school and stays in school for the entire day. In addition, I can provide you with some ways of helping your child go to school with less distress.

Chapter 1 is devoted to helping you understand what school attendance problems are as well as some of the common issues that come with these problems. Chapter 2 is designed to help you understand and determine the main reasons why your particular child is having trouble going to school. Discovering why your child has difficulty attending school is very important because methods of getting one child back to school are not necessarily best for getting another child back to school. We have to treat 6-year-old Jabari, who is crying to be with his mom, differently from 15-year-old Samantha, who is ditching school after lunch and does not want her parents to know where she is. One size does not fit all when it comes to kids with school attendance problems!

Once we know why your child has difficulty attending school, we can then discuss specific methods to help him or her go to school with less distress. These specific methods are covered in Chapters 3, 4, 5, and 6. Although Chapters 3 through 6 are designed for different kinds of school attendance problems, I recommend that you read each chapter. You might find a certain suggestion that applies particularly well to your situation. In Chapter 7, I focus on ways of preventing school attendance problems from happening again and provide suggestions for special circumstances. In Chapter 8, I focus on severe school attendance problems and situations where school has been out of session for an extended period of time.

Will This Book Help Me?

This book will be more helpful for certain families than others (Table 1.1). Let's explore different topics to help you decide whether this book is right for you.

Actual School Attendance Problems

This book will be helpful if your child is actually having trouble going to school or staying in school for an entire day. Parents often ask about their child's refusal to complete homework, inability to make friends or speak at school, and trouble reading. These are important issues that can occur *with* school attendance problems,

Table 1.1 Will This Book Be Helpful to You?

This Book Will Be More Helpful to You If	This Book Will Be Less Helpful to You If
Your child is having trouble going to school or staying in school for an entire day.	Your child goes to school with ease and stays there but has trouble completing homework or listening at home.
Your child has recently started having difficulty attending school.	Your child has had difficulty attending school for a long period of time.
Your child has relatively few symptoms or problems.	Your child has many symptoms or problems.
Your child does not have severe behavior problems.	Your child has severe behavior problems, such as attention deficit hyperactivity disorder, aggression, delinquent behavior, substance use, extreme anxiety and/or depression, or bipolar disorder.
Your child should be going to school but is not.	Your child is having trouble going to school because of some legitimate problem, such as illness or actual school threat.
Your child's difficulty attending school is fairly stable.	Your child's difficulty attending school is getting much worse by the day.
You are sure you want your child to go to school.	You are not sure you want your child to go to school.

but they are not specifically addressed in this book. Instead, I focus mostly on attendance and distress issues. If you feel that issues other than school attendance problems apply to your child, then you may wish to consult a qualified mental health professional (addressed in a later section).

Length of School Attendance Problems

This book will be more helpful if your child has been having trouble attending school for *less than 4 months*. However, this book may also be helpful to some parents whose child previously had problems attending school, like Claire:

> Claire is a 14-year-old girl in ninth grade who is having great difficulty attending school this September. Her parents say that Claire often feels bad when attending school and has already started ditching some classes to be with her friends. Claire had similar problems last year, but her attendance improved after a couple of months, and she had no problems going to school from November to June.

If your child has been having problems attending school for more than 4 months, then you may wish to consult a qualified mental health professional. Suggestions for lengthy school attendance problems are also provided in Chapter 8.

Other Problems

This book is intended for children and families who have fewer and less severe problems. This book will be more useful if your child's school attendance problems are his or her *main and sole behavior problem*. If your child has difficulty attending school *and* has other problems, such as general noncompliance (not listening) at home or lack of friends, or more severe behavior problems like attention deficit hyperactivity disorder or extreme depression, then you may wish to consult a qualified mental health professional. In addition, this book will be more helpful if your family members get along fairly well. You may be "up in arms" about your child's trouble attending school, and this is normal. However, to get a child to go to school with less distress, *parents must be a united team with mutual support.* If you and your spouse or partner seem to be arguing a lot about many things, or if either of you has significant anxiety, depression, substance use, or other problems, then you may wish to consult a qualified mental health professional.

What If This Book Is Not Very Helpful to Me?

If you feel this book would be less helpful for you for the reasons listed in Table 1.1, then I recommend that your family consider seeing a qualified mental health professional. A *clinical child psychologist* has specialized training with youth with severe behavior problems. A *psychiatrist* is a medical doctor who can prescribe medication for severe behavior problems. For many children with severe behavior problems that significantly interfere with daily life, seeing both a clinical child psychologist and a psychiatrist is a good idea.

If you decide to seek a mental health professional in your area, then consult with local people who are knowledgeable about who specializes in certain kinds of problems. Some mental health professionals have special training in substance use or depression. Others work closely with school officials to help resolve problems such as learning disorders, attention deficit hyperactivity disorder, or intense school attendance problems. Consulting with psychology faculty at a local university is a good start when trying to find someone who best fits your situation. If you live in an area where this is not possible, then contact your state associations of psychologists and psychiatrists. In addition, talk to school counselors and other professionals at your child's school who work with certain therapists. You may also consult the websites of national associations of mental health professionals (e.g., https://www.apa.org, https://www.abct.org, and https://www.psych.org).

Difficulty Attending School for Legitimate Reasons

This book will be more helpful if your child *should* be going to school but is still having trouble doing so. The book will be less helpful if your child is having trouble attending school for some *legitimate reason*. Legitimate reasons for not attending school include:

- Medical condition
- Physician or other professional appointment
- Family emergency
- Religious holiday
- Haphazard weather
- School-sanctioned release time for work–study, college, or other educational programs
- Difficult family conditions that prevent school attendance
- True school-based threats to personal self or property

True school-based threats usually include *excessive teasing, taunting, bullying, verbal or physical assaults or intimidation, theft, property damage*, and *sexual or other maltreatment from peers, school officials, or others*. If a child has difficulty attending school because he or she does not want to face these threats, then the threats must be resolved *before* any of the methods in this book are tried.

In this case, parents and school and legal officials should meet to resolve the threat. Solutions may include removing the bully or threat from school and reducing social isolation of the victim. Every instance of bullying must be reported and dealt with swiftly. Children should travel the school with friends, and school officials should better monitor potential threats and actively work to prevent them. If a bullying or otherwise threatening situation is resolved and a child is *still* having trouble going to school, then the strategies described in this book will be more helpful.

In related fashion, some children have trouble attending school because of a *poor school climate*. Youth may complain of tedious curricula, unnecessary homework, and boring or mean-spirited teachers. Other youth are in a racial minority at school, feel threatened by peers or ignored by teachers, suffer overcrowded classrooms, or are frustrated with school regulations that are biased or make little sense. Some children adjust to these situations in different ways, but other children decline to attend school.

A child's complaints about school may be understandable and should be addressed. In this situation, I recommend extended and detailed discussions with school officials (counselors, teachers, administrators) to see what daily changes can be made to enhance a child's satisfaction at school (within reason). Options may include changing class schedules and teachers and curricula (if possible and appropriate), integrating a child into extracurricular activities, setting up school-based incentives, and establishing extra tutoring services. *Accommodation plans* (see Chapter 6) are sometimes helpful in these situations. These plans allow for changes in regular school practices to fit the needs of a particular child with problems that interfere with his or her ability to learn.

Parents sometimes consider switching schools following persistent child demands or requests to go to a new school. *I strongly recommend that you try to resolve your child's attendance problems within your child's current school.* Allowing a child to switch schools is not always the best option because many of the problems at the old school, such as feeling socially isolated, will be present at the new school as well. Switching schools should be considered only as a last resort unless the child's current school climate is extremely threatening, hostile, or unbearable.

School Withdrawal by Parents

Some parents deliberately keep their children home from school, a situation known as *school withdrawal*. Other parents are not particularly concerned about their children's school attendance. Obviously, this book would not be very helpful in these situations.

I assume you are reading this book because you *do* want your child to go to school with less distress and that you *are* highly motivated to help him or her do so.

Why do some parents deliberately keep their children home from school? Common reasons include:

- Babysitting younger brothers and sisters
- Asking a teenager to secure a job
- Hiding signs of maltreatment from school officials
- Protecting children from an ex-spouse or others
- Helping parents with chores
- Punishing the child for some misbehavior
- Trouble on the part of parents to separate from their child
- Excessive conflict with school officials
- Keeping the child at home as a "safety person" if a parent is anxious
- Fear of harm directed toward the child at school

What Difficulties Come With School Attendance Problems?

What are some common behavior problems found in children with trouble attending school? As you may already know, children with trouble attending school are likely to show different kinds of behavior problems. Behavior problems can be divided into those that are *less obvious or clear* and those that are *more obvious or clear*. When a child has difficulty attending school, he may have some of the following *less obvious* problems:

- General anxiety or apprehension or worry that something bad will happen
- Nervousness about being around others or having to perform before others
- General sadness or moping about having to go to school

(Note: Often a child's anxiety and sadness occur together and it is hard to tell which is which; the child may appear cranky, report a sense of dread or "feeling bad" about school, and wish to be left alone. This is common in children with attendance problems, and I talk more about this kind of nervous/sad behavior in Chapter 2.)

- Irritability and restlessness
- Fear of something specific to school, such as a school bus, cafeteria, or teacher
- Physical problems such as stomachaches, headaches, abdominal pain, trembling, nausea, vomiting, frequent urination, muscle tension, diarrhea, dizziness, or fainting. Other physical problems might include heart tremors (palpitations), light-headedness, shortness of breath, hyperventilation, sweating, and menstrual symptoms.
- Trouble sleeping or a feeling of being overly tired, especially in the morning
- Trouble concentrating
- Withdrawal from others

A child with difficulty attending school may also show problems that are *more obvious*, such as the following:

- Temper tantrums, including crying and screaming
- Tearfulness or sobbing
- Refusal to get out of bed or move in the morning
- Noncompliance or defiance to parent or teacher commands or failing or refusing to do as told
- Locking oneself in a room or car to avoid school
- Running away from home to avoid school or running away from the school building
- Clinging to a parent or other adult
- Lying
- Asking the same or similar questions over and over, such as "Do I really have to go to school tomorrow?" "Can't I just stay home?"

or "What if something bad happens?" These questions may come with statements said over and over, such as "I hate school," "I don't want to go to school," or "You can't make me go to school."

- Verbal or physical aggression toward oneself or others to miss school

Do any of these behaviors look familiar to you? Review the lists again and place a check mark next to those that seem to apply most to your child. Does your child show certain behaviors not listed here? If so, then describe them by writing in this space:

_____

_____

_____

_____

If you made several check marks next to the behaviors listed, that's okay. Many children with trouble attending school show many of these behaviors, and these behaviors can even change from day to day! Consider the case of Lindsey:

Lindsey is an 8-year-old girl who has enormous problems getting to school in the morning. Her parents say that Lindsey will not get out of bed until the very last minute and dawdles through her morning tasks until everyone is late getting out of the home. Although this has led to a lot of family arguments, Lindsey says she does not want to go to school because she feels "nervous" and "sick" in the morning and "awful" while at school. When asked why she feels this way, Lindsey cannot say. In addition, Lindsey has been known to have temper tantrums in the morning, cry in the car on the way to school, and even call her mother names for trying to make her go to school.

You can see that Lindsey has problems that are *less obvious or clear* (feeling nervous, sick, and awful) and problems that are *more obvious or clear* (dawdling, tantrums, name-calling). Most children with trouble attending school show less obvious *and* more obvious behavior problems. As mentioned, these problems often change from day to day or week to week.

If your child has trouble attending school and you seem overwhelmed by all of his or her different behaviors, your feelings are normal. We will work on these behaviors together, and I will show you in Chapter 2 how to view your child's behavior in a simpler, easier way. Let's talk more next about school attendance problems.

How Common Are School Attendance Problems? Am I the Only One With a Child With Such a Problem?

Your child is *not* the only one with difficulty going to school. For many years, I have directed a treatment clinic for children with school attendance problems, and parents often express surprise that such a clinic exists or needs to exist! School attendance problems are common. Perhaps a third of children and adolescents will, at some time during their young lives, have trouble attending school. This includes different forms of school attendance problems mentioned previously, such as distress during school, morning misbehaviors, tardiness, skipping classes, and full-day absences.

What Do Children With School Attendance Problems Look Like?

Sometimes it can be hard to tell exactly what kind of child is most likely to have school attendance problems. School attendance problems seem to occur in boys and girls equally and are not necessarily linked to any particular racial or ethnic group. Children who enter a new school building for the first time do seem to be at risk of attendance problems. This includes not only children entering kindergarten or first grade, middle school, and high school, but also children who recently moved from one area to another and who have to enroll in a new school district. Many younger children also have trouble going to school for a full day for the first time.

Any school-aged child, however, such as one in fifth grade who has been going to the same elementary school for years, can have attendance problems. In many of these cases, problems attending school grow more and more intense over the years. Consider the case of Matt:

> Matt is a 10-year-old boy in fifth grade who has missed the past 2 weeks of school. His parents report that Matt's problems attending school actually started in second grade when he cried during much of September, but he seemed to improve afterward. In third grade, Matt's nervousness and anxiety about school lasted until late October. In fourth grade, Matt began missing some school days altogether because he often seemed sick. Most of these days missed were Mondays. Toward the end of fourth grade, Matt made such trouble going to school that he missed the entire last week of school. His parents thought that fifth grade might be different, but Matt immediately started refusing to leave home for school as soon as the school year started.

If your child has been developing greater problems attending school over the years, be assured that this is common. What is most important is to address the problems early before school attendance problems become severe.

How Can I Help My Child Adjust to a New School?

Adjusting to new things can be hard for all of us, and children sometimes have problems managing a new school building or starting school for the first time. Some suggestions follow for helping your child during this tough transition. These suggestions may also be helpful if your child has previously had problems attending school and you are worried that the problems may happen again at the start of the school year:

- Attend all orientation sessions that are held at your child's school before the start of the school year. Be sure to bring your child with you!
- Purchase or secure all necessary school supplies at least 1 week before the start of school.

- With your child, walk around the school so that he and you become *very familiar with* the layout of the school. Show your child his classroom(s) as well as the cafeteria, gymnasium, library, art and music centers, bus areas, playground, and other relevant areas. Ask your child if she has any questions about getting from one place in school to another and address any concerns she has.
- Arrange for you and your child to meet your child's school counselor and teacher(s). Show your child the location of the main office and the counselor's office so that he or she can stop by during the day to ask questions or express concerns.
- Talk to your child about the school bus, including bus number, stops, times, and what to do if he or she misses the school bus. Practice the routine of getting to the school bus stop near home in the morning and at school in the afternoon.
- About 2 weeks before the start of school, have your child begin the morning routine on weekdays as if preparing for school. He or she should arise from bed at a certain early time, wash, eat, dress, brush teeth, and complete other regular morning activities as if he or she were going to school that day. That way, going to school the first day will not be more difficult because of unfamiliarity with the morning routine.
- The night before school starts, have a relaxed conversation with your child about last-minute concerns he or she might have about going to school the next day.
- Plan to make your schedule flexible during your child's first day of school in case he or she is nervous or takes a while to enter the school building.
- Use a supportive but neutral and firm manner to require your child to go to school.

Medical Conditions

As mentioned, many children with school attendance problems have physical complaints such as headaches and stomachaches. Other medical conditions may also be present, such as asthma and other respiratory illnesses. Sleep problems are also frequent. Other common medical problems include influenza, allergies, dysmenorrhea (pain or discomfort surrounding a menstrual period), diabetes, lice, and dental disease. School attendance problems have also been linked to chronic conditions such as:

- *Cancer* (uncontrolled growth of abnormal cells)
- *Chronic fatigue syndrome* (a general condition involving unexplained fatigue, weakness, muscle pain, and trouble thinking)
- *Crohn's disease* (an inflammatory problem often affecting the small intestine and colon)
- *Dyspepsia* (upset stomach or indigestion)
- *Irritable bowel syndrome* (changes in bowel habits involving diarrhea, constipation, abdominal pain, and cramping)

Of course, any medical condition not listed here could also affect a child's school attendance. If your child has physical complaints or medical conditions related to school attendance problems, then be sure to *first* pursue comprehensive medical examinations and treatment. True medical problems must be addressed *before* using any procedures in this book. Do not assume that your child is faking physical symptoms.

A good place to start in this situation is with your family medical doctor or neighborhood children's clinic. Be sure to fully describe your child's symptoms and when they occur. Keep a log of your child's symptoms so you know when they occur and how long they last. Note any symptoms that lessen on Saturdays and Sundays. If your doctor rules out a medical cause for the physical symptoms your child may have, then the procedures in this book may be more helpful.

Some children do fake physical symptoms to try to get out of having to go to school. Illness is a legitimate excuse for getting us out of many obligations, and children learn this at an early age. In addition, some children have minor physical symptoms that are not severe enough to show up on a medical test. These minor symptoms, such as stomach distress, are real, and some children make them seem worse for attention or to try to stay out of school. I talk about how to address these situations in Chapter 5.

What Happens to Children Who Have School Attendance Problems for a Long Time?

As you may already know, a child with trouble attending school for a long period of time may be at risk for certain kinds of related problems. In the short run, these children can become quite distressed. In addition, as a child misses more and more school, grades decline, schoolwork piles up, and friendships become strained or broken. Getting a child to go back to school after several missed weeks can be hard because the child feels overwhelmed by the amount of makeup work that is due and feels isolated from his classmates.

If a child misses a lot of school over the years, then she is at risk in the long run for dropping out of school. Dropping out of school is obviously a very serious problem because doing so prevents the child from securing further education and certain jobs. Studies of adolescents who drop out of school show that, as adults, they often have economic and psychological problems. *However, these consequences do not necessarily apply to everyone who drops out of school.*

What about the effect of school attendance problems on family members? In the short term, a child's difficulty attending school can lead to chaos, distress, tension, arguing, and endless trips to school to meet with counselors, school psychologists, principals, teachers, and other educators. As a child's attendance problems continue, a family may be faced with legal consequences and financial difficulty if work is missed. A sense of helplessness or despair may set in as well, and some children become less supervised.

School attendance problems are discouraging, but you can get your child to attend school on a regular basis and lower his distress level while there. *Doing so will take work on your part and your child's part.* Following the guidelines in this book should help you accomplish what you want to accomplish. However, keep in mind that success for these kids does not always involve full-time school attendance (see Chapter 8).

Defining Success

How do you know if this book worked for you? The most obvious way of knowing that it worked is that your child is back in school and attending full time. In addition, she should be going to school with less distress. However, "success" for kids with school attendance problems sometimes means different things for different kids. For some older adolescents, especially those with long histories of attendance problems, success means that the teenager is enrolled in a modified credit program, alternative high school, hybrid courses, equivalency diploma program, summer classes, and/or school-based mental health services designed to improve school attendance (Chapter 8). If one of these programs helps a child receive a good education and a diploma, then I consider the program to be a success.

What If I Try the Methods in This Book and Nothing Happens?

If you try the methods in this book and they do not seem to help, then one of several things might be happening. First, your situation may not completely fit the purpose of this book, so different or more extensive procedures may be necessary; however, the procedures discussed in this book can still be done under the guidance of a qualified mental health professional, who can help you address intense issues and persistent school attendance problems.

Second, you may have applied the wrong methods for your child. If you think this is the case, then return to Chapter 2 to see exactly what is maintaining your child's school attendance problems. Third, you may have tried the methods for only a short time. The methods in this book have to be carried out for the entire school year. Some parents get their child back to school and then lose a little focus. Instead, parents usually have to practice the methods in this book for at least several months.

Okay, What's Next?

If you feel this book might be helpful to you and that it seems to apply to your situation, then let's get started! I have a couple of things to ask you to do to set the groundwork for what is to come.

Contact Information

The first thing I would like you to do is make a list of relevant names, telephone numbers, and e-mail addresses that you will need. When helping a child get back to school with less distress, frequent communication between parents and school officials is necessary. I would like you to have all contact information at your fingertips. In the worksheet provided (Worksheet 1.1), write the names, main and cell phone numbers, and email addresses for the people listed.

Parent–School Official Discussions

The second thing I would like you to do is to immediately schedule direct meetings with your child's teacher(s) and counselor. You may have already done this, but before using any of the methods in this book, I prefer that you do so again and let school officials know what you plan to do. For a child to get back to school with less distress, *parents and school officials must be on the same page.* In addition, if you have not already done so, speak with school officials about the following types of information:

- Your child's current enrollment status
- Your child's recent school absences (how many, what type, getting worse or better?)
- Your child's course schedule and current grades
- Your child's current homework and required makeup work
- Your child's current behavior in school, including his or her level of distress, interactions with peers and others, and any behavior problems
- School rules regarding attendance, student conduct, and leaving the school campus during the day
- Expected timeline and obstacles for getting your child back to school
- Legal, disciplinary, and other consequences of continued school absences

Some of this information may be needed only one time, such as school policy about ongoing absences. Write down all of this important information and keep it close to you. Feel free to write this information in the blank pages of this book.

Other types of information change a lot and have to be updated constantly. This mostly applies to homework and makeup work. Write this information *every week* in the worksheet provided. Feel free to photocopy Worksheet 1.2 or download multiple copies from the companion website (https://www.oxfordclinicalpsych.com/schoolattendance).

Finally, I have seen many cases of school attendance problems where parents and school officials do not like each other very much. School attendance problems often involve a lot of finger pointing and blame. I strongly encourage you to work to reduce friction with school officials as much as possible. Getting a child back to school with less distress has to be a team effort! Members of the team must work together. If friction exists, then I recommend that parents and educators communicate often and come to meetings with specific ideas for resolving a child's attendance problem.

Worksheet 1.1
Contact Information

Me

_____

_____

My spouse/partner

_____

_____

My child (cell phone number most likely)

_____

_____

Close family relatives who live nearby and others (e.g., neighbors, friends) who can help

_____

_____

My child's school counselor

_____

_____

My child's teacher(s)

_____

_____

My child's principal/dean

_____

_____

My child's school psychologist or school-based social worker

_____

_____

My child's school nurse

_____

_____

My child's school attendance officer

_____

_____

Worksheet 1.2

Date: _____

Homework for This Week   *Current Makeup Work That Needs Completion*

_____   _____

_____   _____

_____   _____

_____   _____

_____   _____

_____   _____

_____   _____

On to Chapter 2

Now that you have everyone's contact information and have spoken with school officials, I invite you to begin reading Chapter 2. There we discuss ways of discovering exactly what is maintaining your child's trouble attending school. Once we figure that out, we can begin to work to fix the problem.

2

Understanding Your Child's School Attendance Problem

In Chapter 1 we discussed different kinds of problems that kids may have when attending school. In this chapter, we begin to solve these problems by first:

- keeping track of, and recording, your child's attendance, level of distress, and morning behavior problems; and
- finding out exactly why your child is having trouble attending school so you know which Chapters (3 through 6) apply most to you.

Tracking and Recording Your Child's School Attendance Problems

One of the most important things to do is to track and record your child's attendance problems. Keep track of your child's actual time in school, level of distress, and morning behavior problems. For the methods in this book to work, you must keep track of your child's behavior *every day*. I ask you to do this for several reasons: Knowing about your child's attendance problems each day will help you, your spouse/partner, your child, and school officials to

- Become more aware of your child's actual time in school, level of distress, and morning behavior problems
- See how your child's behavior changes during the week
- Find out why your child is having trouble attending school

- See whether the methods in this book that you are trying are indeed working
- Exchange more detailed information with one another
- Look for signs that your child's attendance problems may be recurring after the initial problem was fixed

The most important behaviors that should be recorded each school day include actual time in school (attendance), level of distress about school, and morning behavior problems. Let's discuss these separately.

Actual Time in School

If you are reading this book, then increasing the time your child actually spends in school each day may be one of your most important goals. Therefore, we must know how much time your child actually spends in school each day and whether she is going to school more or less than before. Then we can know whether our goal is being reached and what changes we need to make to improve attendance.

You may be unsure about how much time your child actually spends in school each day. Some parents are very familiar with their child's daily attendance because they try to take their child to school each day and see the problems that occur. Other parents are less sure about their child's actual attendance because the child tries to hide behaviors such as skipping classes or leaving school early. Still other parents are completely in the dark about their child's attendance or feel that school officials should be providing them with attendance information. All of these situations are normal, but it's time for a change!

No matter how aware you are now of your child's attendance, *it is very important that you begin to keep track of your child's actual time in school each day.* You may need the help of others, such as a school counselor, teacher, or attendance officer who can communicate with you daily to let you know whether (and how much) your child was in school that day. Perhaps you can arrange a daily time for a telephone call or text with a school counselor, have a school official email you each day, or have a daily report card of attendance sent home each day. Although this takes extra time, communicating in some way with school officials about your child's attendance *each day* is often crucial so that any problem can be dealt with *immediately*, such as the same evening it occurs.

To help you keep track of your child's time in school, use Worksheet 2.1 that is provided. This is a simple document that involves two recordings. In the first column for each school day, record the number of hours your child actually spent in school. If your child went to school the entire day, then you can mark "all" or "full attendance" in the column. If your child missed a certain amount of school time, then be sure this is recorded. Your child may have been expected to go to school on Monday from 9 a.m. to 3 p.m. but did not enter school until 11 a.m. In this case, 4 hours were actually spent in school, so a "4" would be recorded for Monday.

In the second column for each school day, write down whether any partial or full absence from school was *legitimate or excused* ("yes" or "no"). A child may have been truly sick on Tuesday, so a "yes" would be provided in the second column for Tuesday. Be sure to write "yes" *only* if your child was truly sick or was legitimately absent or excused from school for the reasons mentioned in Chapter 1 (e.g., medical doctor appointment, family emergency, hazardous weather).

Finally, at the bottom of the worksheet, write the times that your child should enter school in the morning and leave school in the afternoon. Use these times to help you know what percentage of school time your child is missing. If your daughter is missing 2 hours out of every 6-hour school day, then she is absent for 33% of school time. Knowing these morning and afternoon times will also be useful for improving the morning routine (see Chapter 5) and for checking on your child in the afternoon if she is expected to be home right after school.

You may have a unique situation that does not completely fit this worksheet. Your child may go to school every day but have a lot of distress while there. Therefore, every day is marked as "all" or "full attendance." Or your child may stay in the school building but not enter her classroom (in this case, she is actually in the school building, so count this as a "yes" for now). Or your child has been out of school for quite some time so every day is marked as an absence.

Worksheet 2.1
Time in School

	Number of Hours Spent in School	Legitimate Absence?
Monday	_____	_____
Tuesday	_____	_____
Wednesday	_____	_____
Thursday	_____	_____
Friday	_____	_____
Monday	_____	_____
Tuesday	_____	_____
Wednesday	_____	_____
Thursday	_____	_____
Friday	_____	_____
Monday	_____	_____
Tuesday	_____	_____
Wednesday	_____	_____
Thursday	_____	_____
Friday	_____	_____
Monday	_____	_____

Tuesday   _____   _____

Wednesday   _____   _____

Thursday   _____   _____

Friday   _____   _____

Monday   _____   _____

Tuesday   _____   _____

Wednesday   _____   _____

Thursday   _____   _____

Friday   _____   _____

What time should my child enter school in the morning? _____

What time should my child leave school in the afternoon? _____

Despite these situations, I still ask that you complete this worksheet each school day. As you use the methods in this book, you will find that your child's attendance changes. Some children go back to school or their classroom very gradually, sometimes hour by hour, so knowing how many hours they did so is important. In addition, we always want to know as soon as possible whether any problems arise. If your child suddenly misses more school, and you are immediately aware of this because you have been completing the worksheet, then you can more quickly respond to the problem. Feel free to photocopy this worksheet from the book or download multiple copies from the companion website (www.oxfordclinicalpsych.com/schoolattendance).

Level of Distress Regarding School

Another important goal that you may have if you are reading this book is to help your child attend school with less distress. Therefore, another important piece of information that you and your child should track each day is your child's level of distress regarding school. "Distress" can refer to your child's anxiety, worry, uneasiness, discomfort, nervousness, apprehensiveness, or dread about school. Distress in children is shown in different ways, including crying, clinging, tantrums, irritability, restlessness, withdrawal, and verbal statements about staying home, among other ways. In the space provided next, write down ways you can tell that your child is distressed:

_____

_____

_____

_____

You may use the worksheet provided to record ratings of your child's level of distress about school (Worksheet 2.2). You may photocopy this worksheet from the book or download multiple copies from the companion website (www.oxfordclinicalpsych.com/schoolattendance). In the first column of the worksheet, write your rating of your child's level of distress about school each day. This can be done on a scale of 0 to 10, where 0 is none and 10 is "the worst."

In the second column of the worksheet, ask your child to give you a rating of her distress about school that day. Do not influence your child's answer; her rating may be different from your own, and that's okay! Our goal is to get both ratings—yours and your child's—to lower and more manageable levels. If your child wants to keep her ratings on a separate sheet, that is okay. Your child may also want to keep her ratings private, and that is okay as long as you know that she is actually keeping track of her level of distress every day.

In addition, give separate distress ratings for the morning, afternoon, and evening. Why? Because we want to know the exact pattern of your child's distress during the day so we know exactly how

Worksheet 2.2
Ratings of Distress

	Your rating of your child's distress (morning, afternoon, evening)	Your child's rating of his/her distress (morning, afternoon, evening)
Monday	_____	_____
Tuesday	_____	_____
Wednesday	_____	_____
Thursday	_____	_____
Friday	_____	_____
Saturday	_____	_____
Sunday	_____	_____
Monday	_____	_____
Tuesday	_____	_____
Wednesday	_____	_____
Thursday	_____	_____
Friday	_____	_____
Saturday	_____	_____
Sunday	_____	_____
Monday	_____	_____
Tuesday	_____	_____

Wednesday   _____   _____

Thursday   _____   _____

Friday   _____   _____

Saturday   _____   _____

Sunday   _____   _____

Monday   _____   _____

Tuesday   _____   _____

Wednesday   _____   _____

Thursday   _____   _____

Friday   _____   _____

Saturday   _____   _____

Sunday   _____   _____

Monday   _____   _____

Tuesday   _____   _____

Wednesday   _____   _____

Thursday   _____   _____

Friday   _____   _____

Saturday   _____   _____

Sunday   _____   _____

to handle it. All of following patterns of ratings are addressed in this book:

- Jennifer is distressed only in the morning before school, so her morning distress ratings are usually higher than for the rest of the day.
- Marcus has no problem going to school in the morning but becomes distressed as the day progresses, so his afternoon distress ratings are usually higher than for the rest of the day.
- Mateo is most distressed in the evenings before school, so his evening distress ratings are usually higher than for the rest of the day.
- Sondra is distressed the entire school day, so her ratings usually stay high throughout the day.

You may be asking at this point: What if my child is distressed about only *one* thing? Your child may be distressed *only* about riding the school bus, arriving at the school building, entering a classroom, speaking to or in front of others, eating in the cafeteria, or walking down school hallways. Or your child may be distressed *only* for a 15-minute period before the start of school. If your child is distressed by only one situation, then provide a distress rating during this situation. If your child is distressed only by having to ride the school bus or by another situation, then provide a distress rating for the bus ride or the other situation each day.

You may also be asking: How can I know what my child's level of distress is during the school day? You should be able to rate your child's level of distress in the morning before school and during the evening after school. If you cannot, then talk with others who are around your child during these times and try to make an educated guess about your child's level of distress (or have them provide the rating).

Regarding the afternoon, rate your child's level of distress if she is home from school that afternoon or as she arrives home after school. If possible, speak to your child's teacher or school counselor *each day* or ask to receive a "daily report card" of your child's attendance and distress level. A sample daily report card to be completed by school officials is provided (Worksheet 2.3). You may photocopy this worksheet from the book or download multiple copies from the companion website (www.oxfordclinicalpsych.com/schoolattendance). You may also have to rely on your child's report of her own distress during the afternoon.

Worksheet 2.3
Daily Report Card

Date: _____

Number of hours spent in school today _____

Level of distress shown by child today (use 0–10 scale) _____

_____

Behavior problems in school today

_____

_____

_____

_____

Homework today or other comments

_____

_____

_____

_____

You may also be wondering, Why do I have to give ratings on Saturday and Sunday? First, some children say they are very distressed about school even on the weekends, and *this is a strong sign of true distress*. Second, many children report great distress about school on Sunday evenings, and we want to be sure we know about this. Some of the methods that I discuss in this book are necessary even on Saturdays and Sundays.

Finally, you may be asking, What if my child is not distressed about school but simply won't go? I understand that many children have difficulty attending school even when they are not distressed (we talk about these kids further in this chapter). Some kids skip classes or part of the school day to be with their friends and are not distressed. Even in this situation, I encourage you and your child to provide the distress ratings each day. As your child goes back to school and needs to stay there for an entire day, she may feel some distress when returning. The ratings will allow us to see if any distress is present and then we can address it using the methods in this book.

Morning Behavior Problems

Another important goal that you may have if you are reading this book is to help your child attend school with fewer behavior problems in the morning. Therefore, another important topic to keep track of each day is your child's morning behavior problems. Many families of children with school attendance problems say their morning routine is chaotic, stressful, and full of conflict. We tackle these problems by making the morning routine smoother, predictable, and stress free. First, however, we have to know what is happening.

Children with trouble attending school often show several behavior problems in the morning. You will see a list of these behavior problems in Worksheet 2.4. If your child shows any of these behaviors on a particular weekday (Monday through Friday) morning, then place a check mark next to the behaviors. If your child was particularly clingy on Monday, then place a check mark

Worksheet 2.4
Morning Behavior Problems

	Monday	Tuesday	Wednesday	Thursday	Friday
Refuses to/cannot get out of bed					
Refuses to move					
Will not get ready for school					
Locks self in room or car					
Cries a lot					
Temper tantrum					
Excessive dawdling					
Clings to an adult					
Stomachache or other complaint					
Runs away from home or school					

	Monday	Tuesday	Wednesday	Thursday	Friday
Refuses to/cannot get out of bed					
Refuses to move					
Will not get ready for school					
Locks self in room or car					
Cries a lot					
Temper tantrum					
Excessive dawdling					
Clings to an adult					
Stomachache or other complaint					
Runs away from home or school					
_____					

	Monday	Tuesday	Wednesday	Thursday	Friday
Refuses to/cannot get out of bed					
Refuses to move					
Will not get ready for school					
Locks self in room or car					
Cries a lot					
Temper tantrum					
Excessive dawdling					
Clings to an adult					
Stomachache or other complaint					
Runs away from home or school					
_____					
_____					

next to "clings to an adult" in the Monday column. *Do this each day* and place as many check marks as apply for that day. You may photocopy this worksheet from the book or download multiple copies from the companion website (www.oxfordclinicalpsych.com/ schoolattendance). If your child shows unique morning behavior problems that are not listed on the worksheet, then write them in the following space:

_____

_____

_____

_____

Add these behavior problems to the blank lines on Worksheet 2.4. If your child has no morning behavior problems, then this worksheet is not necessary. Your child may go to school in the morning with no problem but then skip classes during the day. Or she may go to school just fine but is then anxious during classes and tries to come home. These problems will be better measured using Worksheets 2.1 (attendance) and 2.2 (level of distress).

Okay, What's Next?

Please get started *right away* completing the worksheets about your child's actual time spent in school, level of distress, and morning behavior problems. Complete the worksheets *each day* and save them in a binder or folder. As we discuss methods of getting your child to attend school with less distress, we will refer to these worksheets to see if the methods are working. However, completing these worksheets now does not mean we have to wait to do something about your child's attendance problem. We can move straight ahead to discover the exact reason why your child is having trouble going to school. Let's do that now.

Knowing Why Your Child Has Trouble Going to School

Children show many different behaviors when they have trouble attending school (see Chapter 1), which can make the problem seem so frustrating and overwhelming. Isn't there an easier way of thinking about this problem? Yes, there is! A simpler way of looking at school attendance problems is to concentrate on *why* your child has trouble attending school. Helping you find the *why* and then figuring out what to do next are my goals for the rest of this chapter.

Children generally have trouble going to school for one or more of four main reasons. Focusing on these four reasons is much easier than focusing on the many different behavior problems your child may be showing. Once we find out which of these reasons most applies to your child, I can better point you to which direction you should take to resolve your child's attendance problem. Please start thinking about which of these reasons seems to most apply to *your child*:

- To get away from general school-related situations that cause distress (the anxious elementary schoolchild; Chapter 3)
- To get away from school-related social/performance situations that cause distress (the anxious middle/high school adolescent; Chapter 4)
- To get attention from significant others such as parents (the attention-seeking elementary schoolchild; Chapter 5)
- To do fun activities outside of school during school hours (the disengaged middle/high school adolescent; Chapter 6)

The Anxious Elementary Schoolchild

Elementary schoolchildren often have trouble going to school because school-related situations cause general distress for them.

Some children are able to say what causes their distress, and some parents can easily tell what causes their child's distress. Distress is sometimes related to:

- The school bus or car ride to school or getting sick during the bus or car ride
- Missing the school bus
- Entering the school building or classroom
- A particular teacher or other school official
- A particular class or area, such as the playground
- Peers/classmates
- Moving from one area of the school building to another, such as from a classroom to physical education class
- School cafeteria
- Animals, fire alarm, or other specific item

In *most* cases of distress, elementary schoolchildren do not or cannot say specifically what is bothering them. This is very common. Parents and school officials are sometimes frustrated by a child's school attendance problems because the child cannot say exactly what causes her distress. As a result, parents and others ask endless questions that lead nowhere or they have trouble believing that the child is actually distressed.

Your child may be unable to say exactly what is bothering her about school. Why? First, your child may not able to fully describe what it is that upsets her. Some children only know that they "feel bad" at school and do not want to be there. In other words, they are truly distressed about school but lack the ability to describe why in detail. This is normal for young children.

Second, your child may be truly distressed about being in school but for no particular reason. Again, this is normal for young children, and we can work to lower your child's distress even without knowing exactly what it is that upsets her. If you are constantly asking your child to tell you what is wrong and she cannot say, then it is okay to stop asking these questions.

Children with trouble attending school because they are distressed are usually younger, about 5 to 10 years of age. However, any school-aged child could have trouble attending school because of distress. In addition, these children often (though not always) show the following behaviors in the morning and sometimes during the school day:

- Crying or tearfulness
- Anxiety or nervousness
- Sadness or withdrawal from others (usually nervousness and sadness occur together in these children and are hard to tease apart)
- Crankiness, irritability, restlessness, and muscle tension
- Trouble concentrating or sleeping because of school-related distress
- Verbal statements about not wanting to go to school and "hating" it there
- Physical complaints such as stomachaches, headaches, nausea, or other symptoms (see Chapter 1)
- Voice or hands shaking
- Pleas with parents for home-based instruction, excused absences, or future nonattendance
- Fear of some specific school-related object or situation such as an animal

What attendance patterns do these kids usually show? Some children who are distressed about school do in fact go to school but remain distressed while there. For some of these children, their level of distress eventually goes down during the school day, but others remain distressed for most of the school day. Other children become very distressed once their parents bring them to school, and they refuse to enter the school building. Some of these kids will eventually go to school following a battle to get them in the school building, and others will put up such resistance that they are able to stay home from school. Finally, many of these children remain truly distressed about school even on Saturday and Sunday and especially Sunday evening. Consider the case of Joseph:

Joseph is a 7-year-old boy who dawdles in the morning and complains almost every day that he does not want to go to school. He gets up slowly, immediately complains of having a stomachache, cries during the morning, and takes a long time to get dressed. His mother can eventually get him into the car to go to school, but once Joseph is on the school playground with his mother he sobs and says, "I hate school." Despite questions from his mother and his teacher about why he hates school, Joseph only shrugs and says, "I just don't want to go!" In addition, Joseph recently has been complaining in the evening about going to school. This seems especially the case on Sunday evenings.

If Joseph reminds you of your child, then she may be having attendance problems to get away from distress felt at school. Many of these children are not so concerned about being home as they are about being away from school.

Keep in mind that the distress I am talking about here is *not* related to any legitimate reason for missing school. If a child is distressed about school because a bully is threatening her, then the distress is understandable, and the threat must be resolved before the methods in this book are used (see Chapter 1). In addition, your child's distress should be much worse than what is seen for *most kids of her age.* Compare your child to other kids of her age and see whether her distress about school is much worse than theirs. If so, then the methods in this book will be more helpful.

I am referring to children who are *truly* distressed about school and who have trouble attending school even though there is no real reason to feel distressed. If you feel very confident that this reason for school attendance problems most applies to your child, then the methods discussed in Chapter 3 will be most helpful for you. If you are less sure, or feel that other reasons may apply (which may be the case), then please keep reading.

The Anxious Middle/High School Adolescent

Younger children often cannot say exactly what causes them so much distress at school, but adolescents often can. When adolescents are distressed about school, social or performance situations at school are often difficult for them. They worry about making mistakes or being embarrassed or humiliated in front of other people. Some kids worry about being teased, laughed at, or ignored by others. Other kids worry about becoming sick, vomiting, choking, blushing, urinating, or fainting before others. Many of these kids shrink from social and performance situations where they might become the center of attention and judged harshly.

What are social and performance situations? *Social situations* include interactions with others. *Performance situations* include acting in some way before others. Both situations can make youth very nervous or distressed. Common *social situations* at school that cause distress include:

- Starting or maintaining a conversation with other students or adults, especially people the youth does not know well
- Joining a conversation that others are having or introducing oneself
- Asking a teacher or other adults for help
- Interacting with others in a school hallway
- Interacting with others on a playground
- Working with other students on a group project
- Participating in group, team, or club meetings
- Being at assemblies or other large crowds or gatherings at school
- Answering or talking on the telephone
- Setting up dates or get-togethers with peers

Common *performance situations* at school that cause distress include:

- Speaking or reading in front of others in class, such as giving an oral presentation

- Volunteering an answer or having to answer a teacher's question in class
- Writing on a board in front of others, such as solving a math problem
- Taking tests or completing other tasks that will be graded
- Performing in physical education class at school
- Undressing before others in a locker room
- Performing musically in front of others, such as singing or playing an instrument
- Driving before others as in driving class
- Eating in a cafeteria with others
- Using the restrooms at school
- Walking into school or class when others might be watching
- Participating in social events, such as school dances or extracurricular activities
- Having one's picture taken

Youth with trouble attending school because they want to get away from distressing social or performance situations are usually older, about 11 to 17 years of age. However, any school-aged child could have trouble attending school because of distressing social or performance situations. In addition, these youth often (though not always) show the following behaviors throughout the school day:

- Particular anxiety about one class or section of the school day
- Nervousness when around others or when expected to do something in front of others
- Excessive worry about making mistakes or being embarrassed or humiliated
- Skipping particular classes, such as physical education or math class
- Skipping a particular class on a day when a test, oral presentation, or other assignment in front of others is scheduled
- Asking for course schedule changes
- Avoiding situations that involve interactions with others (such avoidance may be obvious, e.g., eating lunch in the restroom, or

more subtle, e.g., eating lunch very near the door of the cafeteria so a quick exit can be made if distress becomes intense)
- Failure to hand in homework or other school assignments because they are not perfect

What attendance patterns do these youth usually show? Some teenagers who are distressed about social or performance situations do in fact go to school but remain distressed while there. Others skip only those classes that make them most anxious, such as physical education class. Still others ditch school for whole sections of the day, such as after lunch or for the entire day. Consider the case of Tyanna:

Tyanna is a 14-year-old girl who has trouble going to school most days because she feels lonely and isolated at school. Being new to this school district, Tyanna has been slow to make friends and often seems uncomfortable in situations where she has to speak up at school. In particular, Tyanna seems to have a hard time answering questions in class and talking with others. Tyanna says she often feels embarrassed at school and that "everything I do is wrong." She is shy and has been skipping her physical education class because she does not want to get undressed before others. Tyanna's parents say their daughter is often sad and anxious on school days but seems better on weekends.

If Tyanna reminds you of your child, then your child may be having problems attending school because she wants to get away from distressing social or performance situations there. Many of these children are not so eager to be home as they are to be away from school.

Keep in mind that the social and performance distress I am talking about here is *not* related to any legitimate reason for missing school. If a child is distressed about school because someone is threatening her, then the distress is understandable, and the threat must be resolved before the methods in this book are used (see Chapter 1). In addition, your child's social or performance distress should be much worse than what is seen for *most kids his or her age*. Compare your child to other kids her age and see whether her distress about social or performance situations is much worse than theirs. If so, then the methods in this book will be more helpful.

I am referring to youth who are *truly* distressed about social or performance situations at school and who have trouble going to school even though there is no real reason to feel distressed. If you feel *very confident* that this reason for school attendance problems most applies to your child, then the methods discussed in Chapter 4 will be most helpful for you. If you are less sure, or feel that other reasons may apply (which may be the case), then please keep reading.

You may have noticed that the first two reasons I discussed for missing school are similar because both involve some level of distress. This means that these children and adolescents are having trouble attending school because they *want to get away from something at school that* is causing them distress. Your child may be having trouble going to school for *both* of the reasons discussed so far, and that's okay. If you feel *very confident* that this is the case, then Chapters 3 and 4 will be helpful to you.

Other youth, however, are not so concerned about getting away from something distressing at school as they are *getting something positive outside of school*. In particular, many children have trouble attending school because they want attention from their parents or because they want to do fun things outside of school during school hours. Let's talk about these two reasons next.

The Attention-Seeking Elementary Schoolchild

Elementary schoolchildren sometimes have trouble going to school because they much prefer to be with parents at their home or work. These children may or may not be distressed about school but are much more concerned about being home from school to get attention from their parents. Many children want to help their parents care for a new baby, complete chores around the home, or go to work with their parents.

Children with trouble attending school because they want attention from their parents are usually younger, about 5 to 10 years of age. However, any school-aged child could have trouble attending school because she wants attention from parents. In addition, these children often (though not always) show the following behaviors throughout the school day:

- Defiance about going to school in the morning, often in the form of temper tantrums
- Stubborn, willful, manipulative, or guilt-inducing behavior to try to stay home
- Verbal statements about wanting to stay home
- Desires for parent to attend school with the child or eat lunch with the child
- Constant telephone calls or texts to parents during the school day
- Constant questions about when a parent will pick up the child from school
- Need for reassurance from parents about the consequences of being separated
- Running away from the school building to try to get home

Many of these children do not say they "hate school" and are instead more concerned about being with their parents. Indeed, many of these kids would gladly go to school if their parents went with them! In addition, many of these kids seek attention from their parents in other ways. Some children resist being left with a babysitter, sleeping over at another child's home, or going to a friend's birthday party without their parents present. Some kids even have trouble sleeping by themselves.

What kind of attendance patterns do these kids usually show? Many of these kids will miss at least part of the school day, usually in the morning as they try their hardest to stay home. As a result, many have a lot of "tardys" or days when they come in late to school. Many times these kids "settle down" after a while in school and attend without any problems the rest of the day. In other cases, though, the child is so resistant that she is able to stay home from school on one or more days. A more serious problem is a child who goes to school but then runs away from the school building during the day to try to get home.

Some children who seek attention from their parents also worry about something harmful or bad happening to their parents. Sometimes, though not always, these concerns follow some major change at home, such as a parent's illness or hospitalization, traffic accident, move to a new area, or conflict or separation between the parents. In addition, these children feel they often have to "check in" with their parents to be sure that nothing bad has happened to their mom or dad. Other children who seek attention from their parents also worry about something harmful happening to *themselves.* Some of these kids worry that they will be kidnapped at school and never see their parents again. Some may have nightmares about being away from their parents or away from home. In addition, they feel they often have to check in with their parents to say that nothing bad has happened to them.

This description implies that a child is distressed but the distress is more about separation from parents and less about school. However, these kids are *not necessarily* distressed about separating from their parents. Instead, many are more *defiant and oppositional* in their behavior to try to be home with their parents. Consider the case of Emily:

> Emily is a 6-year-old girl who has trouble going to school most days because she would rather be with her mother at home. Emily has just entered first grade and seems upset that she has to go an entire school day without seeing her mom. She cries in the morning before school and stomps her feet, asking, "Why can't I just stay home?" Her mother says that getting Emily to school is a daily problem because her daughter is "so stubborn and hard to control." Therefore, Emily's mother started missing work to volunteer in Emily's classroom just so the morning routine is a little easier. However, Emily's mother is worried that she is missing too much work and will soon have to stop going to class with her daughter.

If Emily reminds you of your child, then she may be having problems going to school because she wants attention from you and/or your spouse/partner. Again, many of these children are not as concerned about school as they are about being home with at least one parent.

Keep in mind that the attention-getting behavior I am talking about here is *not* related to any legitimate reason for missing school. If you are in the middle of a difficult custody dispute and your child has legitimate worries about what will happen next, then this situation must be resolved *before* any of the methods in this book are used. In addition, your child's attention-seeking behavior should be much worse than what is seen *for most kids her age*. Compare your child to other kids her age and see whether her attention-seeking behavior is much worse than theirs. If so, then the methods in this book will be more helpful.

I am referring to children who are *truly* seeking attention from their parents and who have trouble going to school even though there is no legitimate reason for doing so. If you feel *very confident* that this reason for school attendance problems most applies to *your child*, then the methods discussed in Chapter 5 will be most helpful for you. If you are less sure, or feel that another reason may apply (which may be the case), then please keep reading.

The Disengaged Middle/High School Adolescent

Adolescents sometimes have trouble going to school because they would much rather be doing fun activities outside school during school hours. These children are not particularly distressed about school, though they often say they are bored there and become disengaged from school. In addition, these children usually *do not want* attention from their parents or even want them to know they are out of school! Many teenagers have trouble attending school because they would much rather be:

- Sleeping late
- Watching movies, playing video games, texting, or engaging in social media
- Playing games or sports with friends who are also missing school

- Riding their bike
- Hanging out alone or with friends at a restaurant or shopping center
- Eating somewhere away from the school campus
- Joyriding in a car
- Attending day parties with peers who are also missing school
- Working at a job

Youth with trouble attending school because they would rather do fun activities outside of school during school hours are usually older, about 11 to 17 years of age. However, any school-aged child could refuse school to do fun activities outside school during school hours. In addition, these children often (though not always) show the following behaviors during the day:

- Skipping classes or large parts of the school day without anyone knowing
- Hanging out with friends who tempt the youth to miss school
- Arguing with parents or others so the absences can continue
- Boredom at school or lack of motivation or engagement
- Constant requests of parents to drop out of school or get a job
- Breaking curfew

What kind of attendance patterns do these kids usually show? Most of these kids will miss at least part of the school day to pursue the fun things they want to do. This may mean skipping school altogether or skipping classes midmorning or lunch to miss the rest of the day. Many of these kids will eat lunch off campus and then decide to take the rest of the day off! In general, they do not want anyone to know where they are, except maybe their friends.

These kinds of attendance problems are more serious than simple "senioritis," where an adolescent close to graduation skips a few classes because of lack of motivation and because the consequences for skipping are not strong ("I'm going to graduate anyway!"). Instead, I am talking about a situation where graduation is far away and the child specifically wants to miss school to be with friends or do fun activities outside of school hours. As a result, his or her absenteeism is serious. Consider the case of Vincent:

> *Vincent is a 16-year-old boy who was reported by his school for missing much of the past 2 weeks of school. Vincent usually goes to school in the morning but often leaves right before or right after lunch. When asked why, Vincent says that his friends come up to him at his locker and urge him to ditch school with them. Vincent says he feels obligated to go and feels somewhat guilty at the time, but then has a good time with his friends during the afternoon. Lately, though, Vincent has been leaving home in the morning and going straight to a friend's home. His grades have started to fall.*

Does Vincent remind you of your child? If so, then your child may be having problems going to school because she wants to do more fun activities outside of school during school hours. Many of these kids are not distressed about school and certainly do not want much attention from their parents. They are usually more interested in being with their peers and are not too concerned about the consequences of missing school. Many have also become disengaged from their schoolwork and from school-based activities.

If you feel *very confident* that your child is missing school *only* to do fun things outside of school during school hours, then the methods discussed in Chapter 6 will be most helpful for you. However, many children who refuse school to do fun things outside of school hours *do* become distressed when they eventually have to go back to school. Therefore, the methods discussed in Chapters 3 and 4 may be useful in this situation. If you are less sure at this point about why your child has trouble attending school, or feel that more than one reason may apply (which may be the case), then please keep reading.

School Attendance Problems for More Than One Reason

As you looked through these descriptions of children and adolescents with trouble attending school, I hope you found one that seems to apply most to your child. If you feel that your child is having trouble attending school for more than one of these reasons, that's okay! Many children do in fact have trouble going to school for different reasons. Consider the following cases:

- Justine is distressed about school and refuses to go and is allowed to stay home from school. She then realizes all the wonderful things that she can do while at home, like play video games! Justine is now having trouble attending school because of school-related distress (the first reason we discussed) *and* because she enjoys fun activities outside of school during school hours (the fourth reason we discussed).
- Armando has been missing a lot of school to be with friends outside of school (the fourth reason we discussed). His parents are now trying to get him to go back to school but he is nervous about (a) facing new classmates and teachers ("They'll wonder where I was and ask a million questions!") and (b) having to finish all the makeup work that has piled up (school-related distress, the first reason we discussed).
- Jessica's parents have recently divorced, and Jessica has been refusing school so she can be with her mother at home (the third reason we discussed). Jessica is often described as a shy, reserved child who has trouble making friends at school. In fact, she says she does not like school because people try to talk to her and that makes her nervous (the second reason we discussed).
- Kong has been having a lot of trouble going to school and staying there for a whole day. He says that he is often upset at school but cannot say why (the first reason we discussed). In addition, Kong has trouble being away from his parents and says that he wants to stay home and play (the third and fourth reasons we discussed).

All of these kids have trouble going to school for *more than one reason*. Again, this is common and still fixable! If your child does seem to be having trouble attending school for more than one reason, then I strongly encourage you to read *all* of the chapters in this book.

Okay, What's Next?

Please start tracking and recording your child's actual time in school, level of distress about school, and morning behavior problems based on the understanding gained from this chapter. *Be sure to do this each day.*

Now we start the hard work of getting your child to go to school and with less distress. Please note that the methods in this book will work only if everyone—you, your spouse/partner, your child, *and* your child's school counselor and other school officials—put in a lot of effort and work *together*.

- If you are *very confident* that your child is having trouble attending school *only* to get away from school-related distress, then Chapter 3 will be most helpful to you, and I encourage you to start there.
- If you are *very confident* that your child is having trouble attending school *only* to get away from distressing social and performance situations there, then Chapter 4 will be most helpful to you, and I encourage you to start there.
- If you are *very confident* that your child is having trouble attending school *only* to get attention from you or significant others, then Chapter 5 will be most helpful to you, and I encourage you to start there.
- If you are *very confident* that your child is having trouble attending school *only* to do fun activities outside of school during school hours, then Chapter 6 will be most helpful to you, and I encourage you to start there.
- If you are still *unsure* about why your child is having trouble attending school, then carefully reread this chapter or read Chapters 3 through 6. You may find in those chapters some additional material to help you decide which reason for difficulty

attending school applies most to your child. You can then use the methods in one or more of those chapters that apply most to you and your child.

Special Topics

Parents often have questions about special topics that will be covered in different chapters. Some of these, such as threatening situations at school, switching schools, making the transition to a new school, and handling conflict with school officials, were presented in Chapter 1. Other special topics include the following:

- Should I medicate my child? (Chapter 3)
- Home-based instruction (Chapter 3)
- When should I keep my child home from school? (Chapter 3)
- My child won't ride the school bus! (Chapter 3)
- Sunday evening blues (Chapter 3)
- What is a panic attack? (Chapter 4)
- Being teased (Chapter 4)
- My child is a perfectionist! (Chapter 4)
- Physical education class (Chapter 4)
- Extracurricular activities (Chapter 4)
- Returning to school after a break or holiday (Chapter 5)
- Should I skip work to go to school with my child? (Chapter 5)
- My child is home from school: What now? (Chapter 5)
- Problems getting out of bed (Chapter 6)
- Accommodation plans (Chapter 6)
- Other special circumstances (leaving work before your child has to go to school, multiple children refusing to go to school, children with developmental disorders) (Chapter 7)
- Severe attendance problems or school has been out of session for an extended time (Chapter 8)

3

The Anxious Elementary School Child

Caleb is a 7-year-old boy who gets up in the morning and immediately starts to cry and say "I don't want to go to school." Although his parents can get Caleb ready for school, their son sulks during the car ride, complains of having a stomachache, and sobs when he sees the school playground. Caleb's mother says she has a hard time getting her son to go into the school building and that she sometimes drives him home when he seems so distraught. Caleb seems fine once home but sulks as well during the evening before school.

This chapter will be *more helpful to* you if your child matches Caleb's situation or if one or both of the following is true:

- Your child is having trouble going to school in the morning because of distress about school or trouble riding the school bus.
- Your child seems quite distressed in the mornings or evenings before school.

This chapter will be *less helpful* to you if one of the following is true:

- Your child is not distressed about school.
- Your child has trouble attending school *only* to gain attention (see Chapter 5).

- Your child has trouble attending school *only* to do fun activities outside of school during school hours (see Chapter 6).

In Chapter 2 we discussed different reasons why children have trouble going to school. One reason is that some elementary schoolchildren like Caleb want to get away from distress they feel when at school. A child's distress may be due to specific things, such as the school bus or walking from one part of the school to another. In many cases, children cannot say what is bothering them, and that's okay. Unless there is some clear threat to your child at school, such as a bully, we do not need to know exactly what is causing his distress. The most important thing is to focus on understanding and reducing the distress and getting your child back in school. Reducing stress and improving school attendance therefore are the focus of this chapter.

Many children with school-related distress are young (like Caleb) or are going to a new school building for the first time. To help your child improve his school attendance and ease distress, I concentrate in this chapter on the following:

- Understanding what distress is: the "feeling," "thinking," and "doing" parts of distress
- Easing physical "feelings" of distress through better breathing and relaxation
- Dealing with the thinking part of distress or what to do when your child says he does not want to go to school
- Managing the doing part of distress by gradually reintroducing your child to school and increasing his time in the classroom

Why Am I Doing This?

If your child resembles Caleb, then he is probably distressed about going to school at some point during the day. Your child may be distressed in the morning before school, upon entering the school building, or for most of the school day. Or he is most distressed about school in the evening before the next school day, especially on Sunday evening. We cover each of these problems in this chapter.

To tackle your child's distress, both you and your child should fully understand what distress actually is. Distress can seem overwhelming and uncontrollable, but the problem can be broken into smaller parts that are easier to understand and control. This will be our first step. Once you know exactly what kind of distress your child has, then we can work to ease his distress and go back to school.

Many distressed children like Caleb have uncomfortable physical feelings, such as aches, trembling, shaking, "butterflies in the stomach," and shortness of breath or hyperventilation (breathing too quickly). To help ease these feelings, we will concentrate on breathing and relaxation techniques that your child can use when upset. These exercises are quick, painless, and easy to use. Many children say they feel more comfortable when they have a way of controlling feelings of distress.

Another major focus of this chapter is to gradually increase the amount of time your child spends in school and in the classroom. There are different ways of doing this, and it is hoped you can find one that will most help your child. Remember that the main goals of this chapter are to help your child be more comfortable about going to school and to stay in school for the entire day. Let's talk next about what distress actually is.

What Is Distress?

Recall from Chapter 2 that "distress" can refer to your child's level of anxiety, worry, uneasiness, discomfort, nervousness, apprehensiveness, or dread about school. Distress in children is shown in different ways, including crying, clinging, tantrums, irritability, restlessness, withdrawal, and verbal statements asking to stay home, among other ways. Your child may also have a unique way of showing his distress; recall that I asked you to write a description of this in Chapter 2.

Distress or anxiety is made of *three main parts*. As you read through each of these parts, think about your description of your child's distress to see which parts apply most to him.

- The feelings part involves uncomfortable physical problems, such as aches, trembling, shaking, butterflies in the stomach, and shortness of breath or hyperventilation (breathing too quickly).
- The thinking part involves uncomfortable thoughts or worries about bad things happening, such as the school bus crashing or everyone laughing during an oral presentation at school. In young children, this part may be shown through statements such as "I don't like school" or "I don't want to go to school."
- The doing part involves avoiding places that cause distress, such as staying away from school or withdrawing from people at a birthday party.

Do these parts look familiar to you or your child? Let's talk about each one in more detail.

The Feelings Part of Distress

Your child may be nervous about school and cries or says "I feel bad" when having to go to school. Parents or teachers sometimes ask a child a lot of questions about what is bothering him or her about school but come away with little information. Part of the reason for this is that *the child is focusing a lot on how he feels inside*. For whatever reason, school has become associated with uncomfortable physical feelings, and your child may be upset mostly with those feelings. Caleb simply could not say what was bothering him about school, but he did complain about feeling terrible when there.

An important thing for you and your child to remember is that everyone feels uncomfortable or distressed from time to time— that's part of being human! Think about situations where you might feel uncomfortable, such as having to confront a cranky coworker or complain about faulty merchandise. Most people who are distressed in a certain situation control their distress and move forward with what they have to do. You may ask your coworker what is wrong or become assertive about returning a bought item.

Other people, however, have trouble controlling their distress and moving forward. Such trouble affected Caleb and is affecting your child at this point. Therefore, we need to teach your child ways to control uncomfortable feelings and to move forward toward full-time school attendance.

Should I Medicate My Child?

Some children have such high levels of distress that their parents wonder whether medication is a good option. *If you are considering medication for your child's distress, then first consult a child psychiatrist who is familiar with the literature on medications for child anxiety and depression.* Several studies have shown that medication can be effective for some children with high levels of distress, and your child may benefit from one of these medications. These medications are designed to help ease a child's physical feelings of distress.

That said, there are some downsides to medication. First, some children with distress do not benefit from medication. Children whose distress is mild or moderate may not benefit as much from medication as children whose distress is severe. Remember that this book will be more helpful if your child's level of distress is mild or moderate, not severe. Second, side effects from medication may occur. Third, medication may help ease physical feelings of distress but may not ease the thinking or doing parts of distress. A child who takes medication for distress about school may feel physically better but may still have thoughts about not wanting to go to school or may still try to avoid school.

If you are considering medication for your child, or if you have additional questions about the issues raised here, then speak with a qualified child psychiatrist and clinical child psychologist (see Chapter 1). Medication and psychological treatment together are sometimes the best way to treat severe distress in children.

A reminder: If your child is distressed about some legitimate threat at school, then the methods in this chapter will be less helpful to you. If he is distressed about the possibility of being bullied, *then this threat must be resolved first*. If a true threat has been removed and your child is *still* having trouble going to school, then the methods in this chapter may be more helpful.

Keep track of your child's level of distress each day by using the worksheet provided in Chapter 2. If you like, you can give a rating for each part of distress: the feelings part, the thinking part, and the doing part. Or you can simply give one rating that involves all of these together. As you and your child practice the methods in this chapter, I will ask you to check whether the methods are working by looking at the daily distress ratings. Remember to record daily attendance and any morning behavior problems as well!

The Thinking Part of Distress

Another important part of distress is the thinking part. When we are distressed or anxious about something, we sometimes think about worst-case scenarios. If a family member is late coming home from school or work, then we may worry that he was in a car accident. This is a normal human experience and one that is usually not a problem: We understand that the worst-case scenario is not likely to have happened. We may shake our head and realize that the odds of the person actually being in a car accident are small, and that other explanations are more reasonable, such as getting caught in heavy traffic.

Some people who are distressed *do* focus a lot on the worst-case scenario and have trouble thinking about other explanations. This also applies to children and perhaps to your child now. A child might assume that others are staring at his skin complexion and laughing as a result. This kind of assumption is not unusual but can be a problem if other, more realistic thoughts are "pushed away." If the child does not think about more reasonable explanations for others' laughter, such as the possibility that others are simply responding to a joke, then he is likely to feel embarrassed or distressed.

Think about when this happens to you. What might you think when a coworker won't speak to you one day? Might you assume that he is angry with you? Sure! But most people also consider other possibilities: maybe the person is having a bad day or is stressed about work and has little time for socializing. When we consider these other explanations, we usually feel better.

Younger children who are distressed *tend not* to have clear thoughts about what distresses them. Despite a lot of parent and teacher questions, these children are not able to say what they are thinking in different situations like going to school. Much of this is due to the child's age—he is simply not at a developmental level where much detail can be given about distressing thoughts. Instead, only general statements such as "I don't like school" or "I feel bad in school" are usually given. Such was the case with Caleb. If this is all you can get from your child, don't be overly concerned. There are ways that you can respond to these statements, and these are discussed later in the chapter.

I cover the "thinking" part of distress more in Chapter 4 when discussing adolescents who are distressed about social and performance situations at school. Adolescents tend to have more detailed thoughts than younger children, so different methods can be used. If your child is younger and this chapter is more appropriate, then feel free to read Chapter 4 anyway; your child will be an adolescent someday!

The Doing Part of Distress

The final part of distress is the doing part or what a child actually does when feeling upset. Most kids who are distressed about school, like Caleb, "do" cry, withdraw from others, and try to avoid school. Other kids might have temper tantrums, scream, and run away from school or home (for this specific problem, see Chapter 5). In most cases, crying and time missed from school are what bother parents the most, so I concentrate on these problems later in this chapter.

As mentioned in Chapter 2, avoiding school because of distress is most common in the morning and especially as a child has to enter the school building and classroom. However, many kids also avoid the school bus or school playground right before school starts. I cover all of these situations.

Your Child's Distress

What does your child feel, think (or say), and do when distressed about school? In the spaces below, write your child's specific feelings, thoughts (or verbal statements), and behaviors when he is distressed about school. If your child does not have one of these parts, such as the thinking part, then go ahead and leave that part blank.

What my child feels when distressed

_____

_____

_____

_____

What my child thinks (or says) when distressed

_____

_____

_____

_____

What my child does when distressed

_____

_____

_____

_____

All the Parts Together

How do all of these parts of distress tie together? In general, one part of distress often leads to another. In other words, there is usually a *sequence* to the parts, and this is likely true for your child as well. When we are distressed, we often have unpleasant feelings and thoughts. These unpleasant feelings and thoughts can then lead to behaviors that cause problems. Recall that Caleb had an unpleasant stomachache (feeling part) and statements about not wanting to go to school (thinking part). The feeling and thinking parts then led to trouble entering the school building (doing part).

Think about someone who is nervous about going to the dentist (Figure 3.1). This person may start to feel physically sick (nauseated, achy) about an hour before a dental appointment. These are the physical feelings of distress. As these feelings worsen, the person may start to think about terrible things that could happen at the dentist's office, such as pain or others' comments about the person's teeth. These thoughts are the "thinking" part of distress. As these physical feelings and worrisome thoughts get worse, the person may be tempted to cancel the appointment. Canceling the appointment is the doing part of distress.

As soon as the appointment is canceled, how do you suppose the person feels? Much better, right? Avoiding something works well in the short term because we feel better: The distress is gone! But is this a good long-term strategy? No. Sooner or later we have to go to the dentist and putting it off only makes things worse. The same is true for your child's distress about school. Avoiding school might seem like a good short-term thing to do because distress is lowered but eventually your child has to learn to cope with stress and go to school.

Think about how you described your child's distress in the morning. What part of the distress starts first? For many children, the feelings part starts first (Figure 3.2). A child may wake up with a stomachache or start to feel generally achy or miserable. As these feelings worsen, the child may begin to say things like "I don't like school" or "I don't want to go to school." At a basic level,

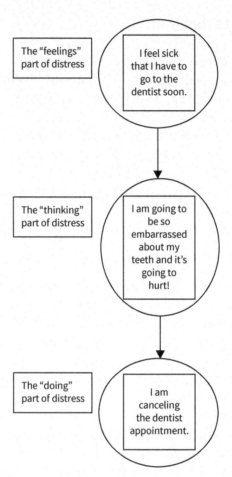

Figure 3.1 Distress diagram (dentist).

these statements are the thinking part of distress. As the feelings and statements continue, or get worse, the child may try to avoid school (the doing part).

Other children show other patterns of distress (Figure 3.3). Some wake up and *immediately* say they do not want to go to school (the thinking part). Then they work themselves up, become very upset, and develop aches and pains as a result (the feelings part). At this

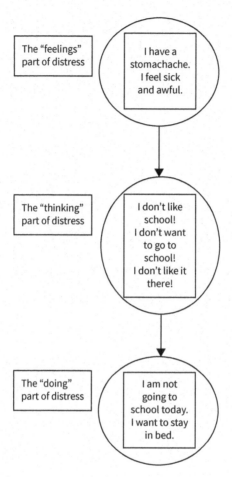

Figure 3.2 Distress diagram (stomachache).

point, they may cry, hide, have a temper tantrum, or have trouble getting on the school bus (the doing part).

Other children begin with certain behaviors first (Figure 3.4). A girl I once worked with (I'll call her Hailey) woke up in the morning and immediately began to cry and say that she did not want to go to school. Then on the way to school she would have problems with diarrhea. In Hailey's case, the doing part of distress started first

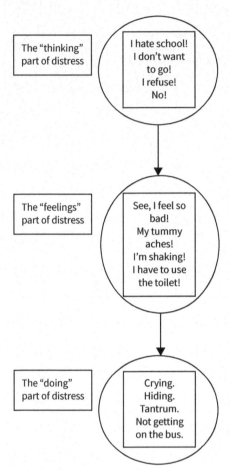

Figure 3.3 Distress diagram (school).

(crying), followed by the thinking part (saying she did not want to go to school), followed by the feelings part (diarrhea).

What pattern of distress best fits your child? In the margins, draw the most common pattern of distress that you see in your child. Feel free to follow the examples given in the figures by drawing circles and arrows and by writing a description of each part. If your child shows different patterns of distress on different days, that's okay. Go ahead and list below all of the different patterns of distress that your child shows.

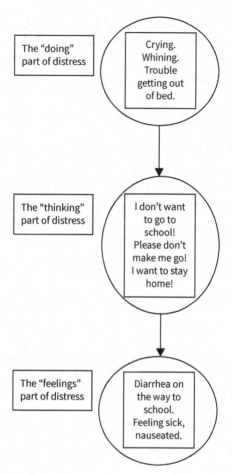

The "doing" part of distress

Crying. Whining. Trouble getting out of bed.

The "thinking" part of distress

I don't want to go to school! Please don't make me go! I want to stay home!

The "feelings" part of distress

Diarrhea on the way to school. Feeling sick, nauseated.

Figure 3.4 Distress diagram (crying).

Changing the Feeling Part of Distress

Now that you have mapped out your child's patterns of distress, see whether you listed any physical feelings that your child may have. If your child has *no* physical feelings of distress, then this section will be less helpful to you (you can skip ahead to the thinking and doing sections). If your child has some physical feelings of distress, then this section will be more helpful to you.

A reminder. Be sure that any physical feelings or symptoms your child may have are not caused by a medical condition. The methods in this chapter will be less helpful if your child's symptoms are caused by an illness or medical condition. If you are unsure, then consult with your pediatrician as soon as possible for a medical evaluation.

There are different methods to help your child ease physical feelings of distress and relax more. A child cannot be physically tense and relaxed at the same time, so we want to make sure that your child is relaxed instead of tense. I discuss three main approaches to ease distress and increase relaxation: breathing, muscle relaxation, and general relaxation. Different children respond differently to each approach, so I encourage you to try each of these to see which one your child likes most.

Breathing

The first method to ease physical feelings of distress is to help your child breathe better. Shortness of breath or breathing too quickly (hyperventilation) can lead to a lot of distress or can be the result of feeling upset. Some children when distressed take shallow breaths or take in only small puffs of air.

Ask your child to first sit in a comfortable position. Then ask your child to practice breathing in slowly through the nose (with mouth closed) and breathing out slowly through the mouth. As your child breathes in, encourage him to breathe deeply into the diaphragm (between the abdomen and chest) or stomach area just below the rib cage. To help this along, ask your child to gently push two fingers into the diaphragm/stomach area to feel the sensation of a full, deep breath (your child's other hand may lie on his or her chest). Ask your child to bring in his stomach when breathing in. Then ask your child to slowly breathe out through the mouth. Practice this breathing method with your child so that he can watch how it is done and you can both learn to relax!

For younger children, creating some image during this process is helpful. Your child may pretend that he is blowing up a tire or is a large, floating balloon. As your child breathes in, he can imagine filling up with fuel and energy. As your child breathes out, he can imagine losing fuel or energy (or tension). The idea here is to control breathing and to help your child understand the difference between feeling tense (after breathing in) and feeling more relaxed (after breathing out). If you like, you can use the following script with your child:

> Pretend that you are a hot-air balloon. When you breathe in, you are filling the balloon with air so that it can go anywhere you want. Breathe in through your nose like this [show for your child]. Breathe slowly and deeply—try to breathe in a lot of air! Now breathe out slowly through your mouth like air leaving a balloon. Count slowly in your head as you breathe out: . . . 1 . . . 2 . . . 3 . . . 4 . . . 5. Let's try this again [practice at least three times]. (Adapted from Kearney & Albano, 2018)

This breathing method is the quickest and easiest method to help your child relax and control physical feelings of distress. In addition, the method can be used at any time when your child is distressed. Even better, the breathing method is one that can be done without drawing a lot of attention from others.

Ask your child to practice the breathing method at least three times per day for about 5 minutes each time. In addition, ask your child to practice this method in the morning before school or during the day at school as he feels distressed. If your child is mostly distressed in the evening before school, then ask him to practice this method at that time. Do not force your child to practice this method if he does not want to. The breathing method will work best if your child is truly motivated to do it.

Muscle Relaxation

The second method to ease physical feelings of distress is muscle relaxation. When children are distressed about school they often feel very tense in their muscles, especially muscles surrounding the hands, face, jaw, and stomach. One way to help your child ease muscle tension is to tense and then release different muscle groups. Try this now: Take your hand and ball it into a fist. Squeeze as hard as possible. Even harder. Hold your tense fist in place for about 10 seconds, then quickly let go. Repeat this once.

How does your hand feel? Many people say their hand feels warm, tingly, and a bit more relaxed. When we tense, hold, and quickly release our muscles, the muscles usually feel looser. This method can be done with other muscle groups as well.

- Bring your shoulders tightly up to your ears, hold them there for 10 seconds, and then release them quickly. Repeat this once.
- Scrunch up your face tightly, hold the tension for 10 seconds, and then release quickly. Repeat this once.
- Bite down hard with your teeth so that your jaw is firmly clenched, hold the clench for 10 seconds, and then release your jaw quickly. Repeat this once.
- Bring in your stomach tightly against your backbone, hold the tension for 10 seconds, and then release your stomach quickly. Repeat this once.
- Tense your legs or push your feet hard onto the floor, keep them tense for 10 seconds, and then release them quickly. Repeat this once.

Try this method with your child. During a peaceful time of day, such as in the evening, ask your child to sit in a comfortable chair while you gradually guide him through different areas of muscle tension and release. Concentrate on the hands, shoulders, face, jaw, stomach, and legs/feet. This process should go *slowly*. Praise your child as he completes each step. If you like, you can use the following script with your child:

(Speaking slowly and in a low voice) Okay, sit down, try to relax, and close your eyes. Try to make your body droopy and floppy, like you are a wet towel. Take your right hand and squeeze it as hard as you can. Hold it tight! (Wait 5 to 10 seconds.) Now let go quickly. Good job. Let's do that again. Take your right hand and squeeze it as hard as you can. Hold it. (Wait 5 to 10 seconds.) Now let go quickly. See how that feels. Nice and warm and loose. Now take your left hand and squeeze it as hard as you can. Hold it tight! (Wait 5 to 10 seconds.) Now let go quickly. Good job. Let's do that again. Take your left hand and squeeze it as hard as you can. Hold it. (Wait 5 to 10 seconds.) Now let go quickly. See how that feels. Nice and warm and loose.

Now shrug your shoulders hard and push them up to your ears. Make your shoulders really tight. Hold them there. (Wait 5 to 10 seconds.) Now let go quickly. Great. Let's do that again. Shrug your shoulders hard and push them up to your ears. Make your shoulders really tight. Hold them there. (Wait 5 to 10 seconds.) Now let go quickly. Great job.

Now scrunch up your face as much as you can. Make your face seem really small and tight. Now hold it there. (Wait 5 to 10 seconds.) Now let your face go droopy. Good. Let's do that again. Scrunch up your face as much as you can. Make your face seem really small and tight. Now hold it there. (Wait 5 to 10 seconds.) Now let your face go droopy. Good job.

Now I want you to bite down real hard with your teeth. Make your jaw really tight. Hold it there. (Wait 5 to 10 seconds.) Now open your jaw. How does that feel? Good. Let's try that again. Bite down real hard with your teeth. Make your jaw really tight. Hold it there. (Wait 5 to 10 seconds.) Now open your jaw. Try to make it as loose as you can. Good practicing!

Let's go to your stomach now. Bring in your stomach as much as you can—make it real tight! Press it against your backbone. Now hold it there. (Wait 5 to 10 seconds.) Now let go quickly. That feels better. Let's try that again. Bring in your stomach as much as you can—make it real tight! Press it against your backbone. Now hold it there. (Wait 5 to 10 seconds.) Now let go quickly. Great job.

Okay, one more. Push your feet onto the floor real hard so your legs feel really tight. Push hard! Now hold it. (Wait 5 to 10 seconds.) Now relax your legs. Shake them a little. Let's try that again. Push your feet onto the floor real hard so your legs feel really tight. Push hard! Now hold it. (Wait 5 to 10 seconds.) Now relax your legs. Shake them a little. Good practicing!

> Now try to make your whole body really droopy: pretend you are a
> wet towel! Relax your whole body and see how nice that feels. You did
> a great job relaxing. Okay, open your eyes. (Adapted from Ollendick &
> Cerny, 1981)

Practice this script *at least once a day* with your child, preferably in
the evening. If you don't have time for the whole script, then concentrate on whatever area of your child's body seems most tense.
Caleb's mother concentrated on her son's stomach area, asking
him to tense and release his muscles there so he felt looser. He
later practiced this method during the school day whenever he felt
uncomfortable.

As your child becomes better able to relax independently, have
him practice the entire script at least twice per day. In addition, ask
your child to practice this method in the morning before school
when he feels most tense. Be sure to praise your child for practicing
muscle relaxation.

General Relaxation

The third method to ease physical feelings of distress involves
breathing and relaxation videos and feedback from you. Many
breathing, relaxation, and yoga videos are available online. Some of
these involve relaxing sounds such as ocean waves, and others involve special instructions about how to breathe properly and relax.
Different children respond differently to various methods, so do
some research and discuss with your child which type of breathing
or relaxation video might be best for him. If you or your child do not
like this idea, that is fine; your child can use the breathing or muscle
relaxation methods described above.

Another important piece of relaxation is feedback from you.
Whenever you notice that your child is particularly tense, encourage him to practice one or more of the relaxation methods
described above. Do not insist upon this or force your child to do
these methods. The methods will work best if your child chooses to

do them on his own or with your help. If your child refuses to practice these methods, then feel free to rely more on the other methods discussed in this chapter.

If your child is distressed for much of the school day, ask your child's teacher to rate your child's level of distress and encourage your child to use the methods described above. Avoid contacting your child during the day or asking that he contact you. The best result is a situation where your child can control his or her physical feelings of distress independently. As your child does so, be sure that you and your child's teacher give a lot of praise.

Changing the "Thinking" Part of Distress

Younger children such as Caleb often do not have detailed thoughts about their distress. Instead, they tend to say things such as "I don't like school" or "I feel bad when I'm at school." So you might be wondering, What do I do when my child says these things?

First, do not use statements such as "Don't worry," "Think happy thoughts," "There's nothing to be afraid of," "You're not really upset," or "You're faking it." These statements do not improve school attendance and can actually make matters worse. If a boy is distressed about school and a parent tells him not to worry, then he will feel even worse when he continues to worry. Or a child may feel that his parents do not believe his statements about being in distress. Remember that your child is truly distressed about school, whatever the reason may be.

Second, do not *constantly* reassure your child. Do not say over and over, "It will be okay" or "You'll be fine" when he is crying or upset. Saying these things once is fine but saying them over and over only rewards your child's statements about not wanting to go to school. I know you want to reassure your child and let him know that everything will be okay *but do this just once*. The rest of the time try to focus on school preparation (see Chapter 5), tell your child to practice better breathing or relaxing, and remind him what needs to be done, such as finishing breakfast. Speak to your child in a neutral and matter-of-fact tone that suggests that going to school is normal and expected.

Home-Based Instruction

Children who do not want to go to school often ask their parents to enroll them in home-based instruction. Home-based instruction broadly refers here to a situation where a child is taught at home by a parent, tutor, or some other adult who may follow a school-based curriculum. Traditionally, home-based instruction was reserved for children with medical or other problems that did not allow them to attend regular school. In recent times, more parents have chosen home-based methods of instruction for many different reasons.

Is home-based instruction right for you and your child? The benefits of home-based instruction include good supervision of the child, increased parent–child contact, and better control over what a child learns. On the flip side, withdrawing a child from school may isolate him or her from social gatherings and peer groups where he or she can build social skills, learn to perform well before others, and develop friendships. In addition, the quality of a child's education at home versus school must be considered.

Home-based instruction may not be a good idea if the *only* motivation is to help a child feel less distress at school. If a child is trying to avoid such distress, then staying home may only reinforce avoidance. A child may even be more likely to avoid other situations in the future. A better method to address avoidance is to practice the skills for managing distress that are in this chapter and in Chapter 4. These skills include learning to relax, thinking more realistically, and gradually facing whatever situation is causing the distress. As a child learns to ease distress, it is hoped school will become a more enjoyable place to be.

Third, do not promise your child extra things for going to school. Some children suddenly become less distressed when their parents promise to buy them something or let them stay up later that night in exchange for going to school. *Do not fall into this trap!* Instead, tell your child that you expect him to go to school and that he can discuss his feelings with you that evening. For now, everyone has to go to work and school.

Finally, please watch your own behavior carefully. Many distressed children also have distressed parents. Feeling nervous yourself is okay except when your child copies the nervousness or copies poor ways of handling nervousness. Some children copy their parents' physical feelings, thoughts, and behaviors of distress. Children also watch how their parents cope with distress and pay close attention to their parents' statements of distress or avoidance of situations. If this applies to you, then set a good example for your child. This means practicing methods of relaxation with your child, refraining from obvious statements about distress, and working hard in the morning to get ready for school or work. In addition, have others praise you and your child for being brave and for tackling the day ahead!

Changing the Doing Part of Distress

If your child is distressed about school but goes to school every day, then concentrate on the feelings and thinking parts of distress that are covered in this chapter. If your child is distressed about school *and is* missing school, then you must also concentrate on the doing part of distress that involves your child's avoidance and absenteeism. The doing part of distress is the focus for the rest of this chapter.

Please note that the methods covered next will require (a) a lot of work on your part and (b) support from others. If you and your spouse/partner work full time, then you will need to make arrangements to accommodate the part-time school schedules we are about to discuss. You may need to arrange supervised child care during the day. Perhaps you have already done this because your child is missing school. If not, then be sure to make these arrangements as soon as possible. Consider extended family members such as grandparents or other relatives as well as friends, neighbors, church members, and others who can help you during this process.

When Should I Keep My Child Home From School?

Parents often ask which physical feelings should keep their child home from school. In general, a child should go to school except when there is

- A fever with a temperature of 100 degrees Fahrenheit or more
- Frequent vomiting
- Bleeding
- Lice
- Severe diarrhea
- Severe flu-like symptoms
- Another severe medical condition or pain

If your child has these problems, then seek the advice of your pediatrician. In addition, I recommend that a child with these problems remain in bed during the school day or complete schoolwork at home. Do not allow your child to do many fun things during the school day because this rewards him for not being in school. If your child is absent from school for more than a couple of days because of these problems, then contact your child's teacher(s) to arrange for homework that she can complete during the day.

I recommend that your child go to school under most circumstances. Minor headaches, stomachaches, or nausea are not enough to keep a child home and might be managed by over-the-counter medication (talk to your pediatrician). If your child's symptoms become more severe during the school day, then he or she can visit the nurse's office. *You will have more success getting your child to go to school if you expect and encourage school attendance every day.* Only more extreme circumstances should keep a child home from school, especially a child with a history of school attendance problems.

If your child is missing school, then he is likely to be (a) arriving late to school in the mornings or (b) missing most of the school day altogether. I discuss each of these problems separately. If your child is arriving late in the mornings, it may be because he is having problems leaving home or entering the school building. Let's talk about this problem first.

Arriving Late in the Morning

Many parents say their child is most distressed just as he enters the school building. Their child may get ready for school with little problem, ride in the car on the way to school, walk to the playground with Mom or Dad, and then the crying starts and he will not go into school. Such was the case for Caleb.

What then? Your first step in this situation should be to inform school officials about what is going on (if they don't already know). Contact your child's school counselor to let him or her know that your child has trouble entering the school building. In addition, tell the school counselor that your child may be late to school but that you will be trying hard to make sure that your child goes to school for at least part of the school day. The school counselor may also help the situation by greeting your child at a certain time and place in the morning and by escorting your child to class if possible. If your child is willing to be escorted into the classroom by a school official, then allow this to happen and leave quickly.

If you can get your child to school but not in the school building, *do not go immediately home with your child.* Going immediately home with your child only reinforces crying and avoidance of school (like canceling the dentist appointment). Instead, stay at the school playground or entrance or sit in your car in the parking lot with your child. Encourage your child to use the methods described to breathe better and relax muscles.

Do not get angry or criticize your child (it's understandable that you may be irritated). Do not say statements such as "Don't worry," "Think happy thoughts," "There's nothing to be afraid of," "You're not really upset," or "You're faking it." Instead, remain calm and speak to your child in a matter-of-fact tone. Let your child vent whatever it is that he is concerned about and tell your child that he is expected to go to school.

If you have to sit or stand in silence, that is fine. Encourage your child every 15 minutes to enter the school building. Even if this goes on for a couple of hours and your child then goes into school, this is better than having your child miss the entire school day. If your child is missing more than a couple of hours of school, then read the next section.

A key rule here is no backsliding! This means that you should not let your child do less than what he has *already shown* he can do. Here are some examples:

- If your son can make it to the entrance or main lobby of the school building, then wait with him there as long as possible and encourage him to go in every 15 minutes. If your child is eventually willing to go to class with a school official, then let this happen and leave quickly.
- If your daughter can make it to a supervised setting such as the school counselor's office or school library, then escort her there and have her remain there for some time before entering class. If possible, leave the school building and allow your child to be escorted to class by a school official.
- If your son can make it into the classroom after some period of time, even if he is late, then allow him to do so (then read the next section).

If your child has problems getting ready for school in the morning, see Chapter 5 for recommendations on structuring the morning routine. If your child is missing most of the school day, then read the next section.

Missing Most of the School Day

If your child is distressed about school and is missing most of the school day, then we must arrange a gradual schedule of returning him to school. Because your child may feel overwhelmed by attending the entire school day, and because we want your child to practice the methods described earlier in this chapter, a *part-time attendance schedule* may be what we have to aim for first. There are different ways of doing this that are described in the next sections. Of course, the eventual goal of this approach is full-time attendance with little distress.

Before starting a part-time attendance schedule, *you must meet with relevant school officials* to plot a course that is acceptable to both you and them. Key school officials would be the school counselor, school psychologist, or principal (you should have their contact information ready; Chapter 1). Find out who you need to visit to put a part-time schedule in place. In addition, explain to this person why you are doing so: to gradually get your child more used to school while easing his physical feelings of distress.

Adding One Step at a Time

If your child is missing most of the school day, then the first step toward full-time school attendance should be small. Think about what time of day might be easiest for your child to go to school. This could be in the morning or afternoon, at lunchtime, or maybe for a couple of classes such as science and band. Once you know what time of day your child is most likely to go to school, this might give you an idea about where to start. Of course, input from school officials is important as well.

The first step in a part-time schedule can involve one of the following:

- Your child goes to school in the morning and is then allowed to come home within an hour (then you gradually work forward by adding more time).
- Your child goes to school at 2 p.m. and is then allowed to come home when school normally ends, say at 3:10 p.m. (then you gradually work backward by adding more time).
- Your child goes to school only for lunch and is then allowed to come home afterward (then you gradually add more school time before and after lunch).
- Your child goes to school only for his favorite class or time of day (then you gradually add more classes or school time).

- Your child attends a schoolroom other than his classroom, such as the school library, school counselor or nurse's office, or main lobby (then you gradually add more classroom time).

Let's discuss each of these approaches separately. *As you try one of these approaches, be sure to keep track of your child's daily attendance by using the worksheet provided in* Chapter 2. Doing this will allow you to see if what you are doing is working or if another approach is needed. Try not to switch your approach unless you have tried it for at least 1 week and preferably 2 weeks. If one approach is not working after a couple of weeks, then a different one may be tried. Be sure to consult with your child's school counselor or other school officials during this process. Also, always let your child know in advance what the plan is for the next school day.

Morning

Younger children usually respond best to a part-time schedule that involves some morning classroom time before they are allowed to come home. If you choose this option, then tell your child that he is expected to go to school and that you (or someone) will pick him or her up at 10 a.m. (then be sure to do this!). If your child does go to school with little problem under this condition, then give a lot of praise. When your child is home the rest of the day, require him to complete schoolwork that you collected from your child's teacher. If your child has completed all of his schoolwork or none was sent home, then require that he continue to do academic tasks such as read books, practice multiplication tables, or tackle educational games on the computer.

Do not let your child do fun things during regular school hours. If your child did go to school as planned (even if for the hour) *and* completed academic tasks during the day, then he can be allowed to play or do other fun things *after* school hours. If your child did not go to school as planned or did not complete academic tasks during the day, then ask your child to work around the home, send him to bed early, and say that you expect better behavior the next day (for more detailed information about rewards and disincentives, see Chapter 5).

Track your child's level of distress each day (see Chapter 2). Once your child's level of distress is low when attending school for an hour, another hour can be added. How do you know if distress has been lowered enough? I recommend that the distress level at each step at least be cut in half. So, if your rating of your child's distress averages about an "8" every day, then wait until the distress level is "4" or less before going on to the next step. If your child still seems quite distressed after some period of time, say more than a week, then perhaps the time that he is in school is too long. If so, reduce it a bit, perhaps to 30 minutes, *but still require your child to go to school.*

If your child's distress level becomes low rather quickly, which sometimes happens, then go to the next step. The next step can be adding another hour to the school day; in this case, you may pick up your child from school at 11 a.m. instead of 10 a.m. The rest of the day should then go as discussed above. Once your child has mastered this step, add an hour at a time until he can go to school for the entire day. Be sure to keep rating his level of distress and talk to your child and his teacher(s) to be sure that distress has been truly lowered.

If your child misses the hour of school that was scheduled, then keep trying during the school day to get that hour of attendance (see previous section). If necessary, sit with your child at school or in the car at school and encourage him every 15 minutes to enter the school building. Be sure that your child practices the methods described earlier to ease physical feelings of distress. *Remember: no backsliding!* If your child has shown that he can go to school for at least 2 hours, then this is the minimum amount of school that he should attend.

Afternoon

Other children find it easier to go to school in the afternoon and gradually add more time to school by working backward. A child may be expected to go to school at 2 p.m. and then be allowed to come home as school normally ends, say at 3:10 p.m. In this case, the same gradual process of adding school applies. Once a child can go to school from 2 to 3:10 p.m. with little distress, then an hour can be added (so, 1 to 3:10 p.m.). This is continued until full-time school attendance is achieved. During the day up to formal school attendance, your child should complete schoolwork or other academic tasks.

The downside of using this schedule, as you might imagine, is that it leaves little room for error. If your child refuses to go to school at 2 p.m., then there is little time left to salvage at least some school attendance (unlike in the morning, where you can keep trying for a whole day to get at least some attendance). Therefore, consider the afternoon option very carefully and perhaps as a last resort. This option is probably best for children whose parents are very confident that they will follow through with instructions to go to school in the afternoon.

My Child Won't Ride the School Bus!

Many children who are distressed about school do miss school, but others simply have problems riding the school bus. If your child has problems riding the school bus, then it may be due to worry about becoming sick or getting closer to school. In other cases, children cannot say why they get distressed on the school bus—they just do!

If your child has this problem, then ask him to take just a short trip on the school bus. This may involve simply standing at the school bus stop, getting on the bus, and then stepping off before you drive him to school. Or your child may get on the school bus and ride it to a next stop that may be just a minute or so away. As your child does this, be sure that he practices the methods to ease distress that I cover in this chapter. In addition, rate your child's level of distress during each step using the worksheet given in Chapter 2.

As your child masters these early steps, gradually increase the length of time that she rides the bus. This may involve riding for a longer period of time or arriving at more stops (perhaps add one stop every 2 days). Praise your child for doing each step successfully. Try to get to the point where your child can ride the bus all the way to school with you driving behind the bus.

At this point, work backward. When your child is 5 minutes away from school, drive away and let her finish alone (you can tell your child in advance about this). Once she can handle this, then gradually increase the amount of time that he is riding without you following behind. Give your child a lot of praise when she can finally make it there alone!

Lunch

Another part-time school attendance option is to start at lunchtime and work from the middle of the day outward. In this case, require your child to eat lunch with his classmates, which is often an enjoyable and less distressing time. The advantage of this approach is that the child is exposed to at least part of the school day and will likely interact with peers who will encourage your child to go to class. If you choose this option, then your child is first expected to attend lunch *only*. He can complete schoolwork or other academic tasks during the morning and afternoon at home.

Once your child can eat lunch at school with ease, gradually increase classroom time just before and just after lunch. A good place to start is 30 minutes before lunch and 30 minutes after lunch. So, if your child has lunch from noon to 12:30 p.m., require that he be in the classroom from 11:30 a.m. to noon and from 12:30 to 1:00 p.m. As your child is better able to handle this schedule, gradually increase the amount of time in class until full-time attendance is achieved.

Favorite Time of Day

Some kids tell me they would be willing to go to school if they only had to go to science class. So, I tell them: Go to science class! *Attending school for at least one class or for at least part of the school day is far better than no attendance at all.* If your child is in this category, then require him to go to the classes he likes best. Once your child is attending this class regularly with little distress, then his second-favorite class can be added. Once your child is attending these two classes regularly with little distress, then his third-favorite class can be added, and so forth. *Remember: no backsliding!* Once your child has shown that he can attend a certain number of classes, then this is the minimum amount of time he should be in school each day.

Some parents ask whether switching a child's classes is a good idea. If the "switching around" involves just a class or two, this is usually not a problem. But, if your child wants his entire schedule changed, he may be delaying the process of going back to school. Work with your child's school counselor to "tweak" your child's schedule if necessary but make it clear to your child that he is expected to attend school full-time eventually and no matter the schedule.

Attending School But Outside the Classroom

Other kids can easily enter their school building but not their classroom. If your child matches this situation, then arrange with school officials so that he attends school in some supervised setting outside the classroom. Your child may spend the day in the school library doing schoolwork or helping the librarian. Or he may sit in the main, counselor's, or nurse's office during the day. Each of these scenarios is much better than being home all day.

As your child becomes more used to being in the school building, and becomes more relaxed and less distressed, gradually increase the amount of time that he spends in the classroom. This may involve small steps such as an hour at a time or larger steps such as a morning or afternoon (whatever your child can handle at that time and what the school will allow). If your child is very resistant about going into the class, then arrange to have a couple of his classmates (or the entire class) visit your child and encourage him to come to class. The classmates can say what interesting things they are doing or that they miss your child. Obviously these suggestions require a lot of cooperation from school officials, so make sure everyone is "on board" before beginning.

Sunday Evening Blues

When children finally go back to school, some are still a bit distressed on Sunday evenings before the start of the school week. If your child is distressed in the evenings before school, particularly on Sunday evening, then be sure to talk to him about his concerns. Be supportive but make it clear that he is expected to go to school the next day. Ask your child to practice the breathing and relaxation methods described in this chapter. In addition, if your child is focused on the entire school week, then encourage him to focus on going to school just one day at a time. After all, your child's teacher can't cram a whole week of school into Monday!

Another idea is to plan a fun family get-together on Sunday afternoon but allow your child to rest comfortably Sunday evening. Planning something small but special on Monday evening is also a good idea so that your child has something to look forward to. Examples include staying up 20 minutes later for going to school on time that morning, enjoying a favorite dessert, or playing a game with Mom.

As you talk to your child during the week, praise even minor things such as entering the school building, crying less, and being brave. In addition, point out to your child how going to school helps Mom and Dad. Knowing that you appreciate your child's effort will go a long way toward making the morning seem less dreadful and will help motivate her to keep going to school.

Do's and Don'ts!

I know that I have given you a lot of information in this chapter. Here is a list of some do and don't reminders:

Do:

- Help your child understand the different parts of distress: the physical feelings, thinking, and doing parts of distress.
- Think about how these different parts of distress occur in your child.
- Teach your child better breathing by using deep, slow, diaphragmatic breathing.
- Teach your child to relax his muscles using the tense-and-release method.

- Encourage your child to relax in general and give him feedback about doing so.
- Speak to your child in a calm, matter-of-fact tone.
- Expect your child to go to school each day.
- Work closely with school officials when developing your plans.
- Wait at school with your child as long as possible.
- Set up a part-time school attendance schedule if necessary.
- Seek support from others.
- Be consistent and use these methods every day.

Don't:
- Argue, yell, lecture, criticize, negotiate, beg, or bribe your child to go to school.
- Ignore your child's distress.
- Use statements such as "Don't worry," "Think happy thoughts," "There's nothing to be afraid of," "You're not really upset," or "You're faking it."
- Linger at school or the playground when your child goes to class.
- Allow your child to come home early or do fun things during school hours.

Other Skills

Anxious elementary schoolchildren sometimes lose ability in certain skills if they have missed a lengthy time at school. These skills can include asking and answering questions in class, completing and handing in homework independently, managing negative feedback or comments from others, handling difficult or unpredictable situations, solving problems independently, or speaking to classmates at school. If this is the case for your child, then work with school officials to improve these skills or seek consultation from a qualified mental health professional (see Chapter 1).

Final Comments

Having a child who is distressed about school and who is missing school can be very upsetting, but the problem is fixable! Easing a child's distress and getting him back into school is best accomplished with a lot of persistence, patience, structure, support from others in your life, and cooperation with school officials who can help. You can do it!

4

The Anxious Middle/High School Adolescent

Raven is a 13-year-old girl who has problems attending school because she is nervous in different social and performance situations at school. Raven has skipped several classes already this year and has three full-day absences. She says she is shy, feels uncomfortable talking to other kids at school, and does not like speaking before others or going to physical education class. She has been skipping classes where she has to take tests or give oral presentations, and her teachers complain that Raven will not answer questions in class.

This chapter will be *more helpful* to you if your child matches Raven's situation or if one or both of the following is true:

- Your child is having trouble going to school or classes because of distress about social or performance situations at school.
- Your child is missing certain classes, such as physical education, choir, band, reading, English, or other courses where performing before others is expected.

This chapter will be *less helpful* to you if one of the following is true:

- Your child is not distressed about school.
- Your child is refusing school *only* for attention (see Chapter 5).

- Your child is missing school *only* to do fun activities outside of school during school hours (see Chapter 6).

In Chapter 2 we discussed different reasons why children and adolescents have trouble going to school. One reason is that some teenagers like Raven want to get away from distress they feel when talking to others (*social situations*) or when performing in front of others (*performance situations*). Raven was somewhat shy and had problems talking to other kids at school. In particular, she had trouble starting conversations or keeping conversations going. In addition, she did not like the spotlight to be on her, so she was nervous when she felt others were watching her do something like answer a question in class, change clothes in the locker room, or give an oral report (see Chapter 2 for more examples). As a result, she sometimes avoided classes or other situations at school where these things occurred.

If you read Chapter 2 or 3, you learned that many younger children are distressed about school but cannot say what bothers them. Teenagers like Raven, however, are better able to describe the distress they feel at school and what bothers them there. Teenagers often say their distress about school is due to social or performance situations. Knowing about these situations is good because it gives us specific goals, such as helping your child talk to others or give an oral presentation in class. If your child is missing school, then easing her distress in these situations will also help improve school attendance.

The main goals of this chapter are to help your teenager be less distressed in social and performance situations and to improve her school attendance. To do so, I concentrate on the following:

- Understanding what distress is: the "feeling," "thinking," and "doing" parts of distress
- Easing physical feelings of distress
- Dealing with the thinking part of distress, or how to help your child think more realistically in social or performance situations
- Managing the doing part of distress by monitoring your child's school attendance and increasing her time in the classroom.

If you read Chapter 3, then you might be wondering how this chapter is different. Yes, there are some similarities between what I recommend for younger children with general distress (Chapter 3) and what I recommend for older children and adolescents with social and performance distress (this chapter). Because older kids with social and performance distress often have more detailed thoughts, the thinking part of distress receives a lot more attention in this chapter.

Why Am I Doing This?

If your child resembles Raven, then she is distressed about different social or performance situations at school. Your child may be distressed about these situations in the morning before school, during the school day, or perhaps in the evening before the next school day. Your child may talk a lot about her distress or be kind of quiet about it. That's okay.

To tackle your child's distress, both you and your child should understand what distress actually is. As mentioned in Chapter 3, distress can sometimes seem overwhelming and uncontrollable. However, distress can actually be broken into smaller parts that are easier to understand and control. This will be our first step. If you think this chapter applies to your older child or adolescent, then I *strongly encourage* you to involve her in reading this chapter and discussing its contents.

Many children who are distressed have uncomfortable physical feelings, such as trembling, shaking, "butterflies in the stomach," and shortness of breath or hyperventilation (breathing too quickly). To ease these feelings, we concentrate on better breathing and relaxation techniques that your child can use when upset. These exercises are quick, painless, and easy to use. Many children say they feel more comfortable when they have a way to control these distressing feelings.

A main focus of this chapter is to change the way your child *thinks* about different social or performance situations. Many older children and adolescents wrongly believe that terrible, catastrophic things will happen in different social and performance situations. As a result, they avoid these situations and miss school. One focus of this chapter is to help your child think more realistically in these situations.

Another major focus of this chapter is to gradually increase the amount of time your child participates in social and performance situations at school. As your child becomes more comfortable and confident in these situations, her school attendance is also likely to improve. Remember that the main goals of this chapter are to help your child be more comfortable about going to school and to stay in school for the entire day. Let's talk next about what distress actually is.

What Is Distress?

Recall from Chapter 2 that "distress" can refer to your child's level of anxiety, worry, uneasiness, discomfort, nervousness, apprehensiveness, or dread about school. Distress in children is shown in different ways; older children and adolescents often have avoidance, withdrawal, sadness, noncompliance, irritability, restlessness, and requests to stay home. Your child may also have a unique way of showing her distress, and you should keep this in mind as we go along.

Distress or anxiety is made of *three main parts*:

- A feelings part that involves uncomfortable physical problems such as trembling, shaking, butterflies in the stomach, and shortness of breath or hyperventilation (breathing too quickly)
- A thinking part that involves uncomfortable thoughts or worries about bad things happening, such as everyone laughing as a child changes clothes in a locker room or tripping over words during an oral presentation at school
- A doing part that usually involves moving away from something that causes distress, such as avoiding school or withdrawing from people at a social gathering

Do these parts look familiar to you or your child? Let's talk about each one in more detail.

The Feelings Part of Distress

Your child may be nervous about social or performance situations at school and is quite upset when in school. When older children and adolescents are distressed about speaking to others or performing in front of others, they often have uncomfortable physical feelings such as trembling, shaking, muscle tension, or breathing problems.

As I mentioned in Chapter 3, feeling uncomfortable in certain situations is common and affects everyone. An important thing for you and your child to remember is that everyone gets distressed from time to time—that's part of being human! I encourage you to talk to your child about situations that make different people in your lives nervous or distressed. Think about how Mom may not like to confront a mechanic about getting a car fixed, how Dad may not like to ask people for directions, and how Uncle Joe doesn't like to go to wedding receptions (yes, a little stereotypical here). The point is that everyone feels uncomfortable in different situations from time to time, and your child is no different.

Most people who are distressed in certain situations are able to control their distress and move forward with what they have to do. Uncle Joe may understand that Aunt Jo really wants him to go to the wedding reception, so he "puts aside" his nervousness and goes. Other people, however, including your child at this point, have trouble controlling their distress in these situations. We need to teach your child ways to control uncomfortable feelings and to move forward toward full-time school attendance.

A reminder: If your child is distressed about some legitimate threat at school, the methods in this chapter will be less helpful to you. If she is distressed about the possibility of being bullied, *then this threat must be resolved first*. If a true threat has been removed and your child is *still* having trouble going to school, then the methods in this chapter may be more helpful.

Keep track of your child's level of distress each day by using the worksheet provided in Chapter 2. If you like, you can give a rating for each part of distress: the feelings part, the thinking part, and the doing part. Or you can simply give one rating that involves all of these together. As you and your child practice the methods in this chapter, I will ask you to check whether the methods are working by looking at the daily distress ratings. Don't forget to record daily attendance and any morning behavior problems as well!

The Thinking Part of Distress

Another important part of distress is the thinking part. When we are distressed or anxious about something, we sometimes think about worst-case scenarios or all the terrible things that could happen to us. When we have to give a toast or speak before others, we might be nervous about making a mistake, tripping over our words, or seeing people snicker. Sometimes these thoughts can be so bad that we avoid these situations.

Worrying about things is also a normal human experience; we all worry about something! But worry is not usually a problem because we understand that horrible things are not likely to happen. We may be nervous about giving a toast at a party, but we do it anyway because we are surrounded by family and friends who are not likely to ridicule us!

As mentioned in Chapter 3, some people who are distressed focus a lot on the *worst-case scenario* and have trouble thinking about *other* explanations. This applies to children and adolescents as well. A teenager might assume that others in a locker room are staring at her body and laughing when in fact they are joking about something else. This kind of thought is not unusual, but it can be a problem if other thoughts are "pushed away." If the teenager fails to think about more reasonable explanations for what just happened, such as the possibility that others are simply laughing at a joke, then she is likely to feel distressed and may even skip her physical education class.

Think about when this happens to you. What might you think when a coworker won't speak to you one day? Might you assume that he or she is angry with you? Sure! But most people also consider other possibilities: Maybe the person is having a bad day or is stressed about work and has little time for socializing.

What Is a Panic Attack?

Some parents say their children have "panic attacks" because the children (and sometimes the parents!) feel very distressed or anxious for long periods of time, such as 3 to 4 hours. But being generally distressed *does not necessarily mean* that one is having a panic attack. Instead, a panic attack involves a *short period of time*, often less than 15 minutes, in which a person suddenly and for little reason experiences many physical feelings and becomes terrified. These physical feelings usually include increased heart rate (feeling of heart "pounding"), sweating, shaking, hot flashes, shortness of breath, nausea, dizziness, chest pain, trouble swallowing, and numbness or tingling sensations.

With these physical feelings often come thoughts or worries about dying, losing control, or going crazy. Panic attacks usually start very suddenly and often without warning but end just as quickly. Panic attacks themselves are *harmless*, but people with panic attacks often worry that the physical feelings are dangerous (they're not). In addition, many people with panic attacks eventually avoid different public situations because they are afraid of having a panic attack and being humiliated as a result.

If your child is generally distressed about school, he or she is not likely having a panic attack. General worry or distress that lasts for a while is different and is the focus of this chapter. Also, panic attacks are unusual in children younger than age 13 years. However, some teenagers do have panic attacks. If you feel that your child is having specific and severe panic attacks related to school, then the methods in this book will be less helpful to you. Instead, seek the help of a qualified mental health professional who is experienced in treating panic attacks (see Chapter 1).

Older children and adolescents who are distressed about social or performance situations at school tend to focus on worst-case scenarios or worry that terrible, catastrophic things are going to happen. They think about all the possible things that could go wrong and how bad they will feel. In particular, they often worry about:

- Being embarrassed or humiliated before others
- Being laughed at or ridiculed in some way
- Blushing or appearing very nervous before others
- Being excluded from some social group, such as a clique of friends
- Being ignored by others when speaking or asking for help

Having these thoughts or worries often leads to avoidance and difficulty attending school—this is the doing part of distress that I cover next.

Being Teased

Many kids have trouble going to school because they are teased by other kids. Teasing can be especially hurtful if directed toward sensitive areas such as weight or skin complexion. In addition, teasing can be very harmful if it is part of bullying or more serious threats. Consult with school officials to seek resolution of the problem.

Mild teasing is common among children, but your child may be especially sensitive to it and not want to attend school as a result. I recommend that children not respond to teasers. Some children can deflect teasing by teasing back or by laughing it off but other kids are very bothered by teasing, so I encourage them to simply ignore any insults. Do not have a child respond to provocation. Most teasers are looking for some reaction and usually move on if they do not get a reaction. If your child is being teased, then have her practice the breathing exercise (see Chapter 3) and continue doing what she was doing before. If the teasing gets worse, then advise her to walk away or seek the comfort of friends.

If this does not work, then ask your child to speak to an adult who can help at school. Children sometimes do not like talking to adults at school about other kids, but school should be a safe and comfortable place to learn. School officials are generally sensitive to these concerns, so encourage your child to speak to them when he feels threatened or when his personal space is violated. In addition, be sure to discuss the situation with your child each evening.

The Doing Part of Distress

The final part of distress is the doing part or what a child actually does when upset or worried that bad things will happen. Many older children and adolescents like Raven who are distressed about school "do" try to avoid school, skip classes, or withdraw from others. In most cases, worrisome thoughts and time missed from school are what concern parents the most, so I concentrate on these problems later in this chapter.

As mentioned in Chapter 2, avoiding school because of social or performance distress is most common during the day at school and especially in classes where a teenager is expected to do something in front of others. However, many kids also avoid the entire school day if they are particularly nervous about interacting with other kids.

What does your child feel, think (or say), and do when distressed about school? In the spaces below, write your child's specific feelings, thoughts (or statements), and behaviors when she is distressed about school. If your child does not have issues with one of these parts, then leave that part blank.

What my child feels when distressed

_____

_____

_____

_____

What my child thinks (or says) when distressed

_____

_____

_____

_____

What my child does when distressed

_____

_____

_____

_____

All the Parts Together

We experience feelings and thoughts that are unpleasant when we are distressed. These unpleasant feelings and thoughts then lead to behaviors that cause problems. Someone who is nervous about talking to unfamiliar people at a party may feel physically sick or "shaky" an hour before the party (Figure 4.1). As these feelings worsen, the person may start to think about all the terrible things that could happen at the party, such as feeling isolated or hearing comments about her dress or behavior ("Why isn't she talking to anyone?"). As physical feelings and worrisome thoughts get worse, the person may be tempted to avoid the party (the doing part).

As soon as the person avoids the party and jumps on the couch at home, how do you suppose she feels? Much better, right? Avoiding something works well in the short term because we feel better—the distress goes away! But is this a good long-term strategy? No. Sooner or later we have to interact with other people and socialize, and putting it off only makes things worse. The same is true for your child's

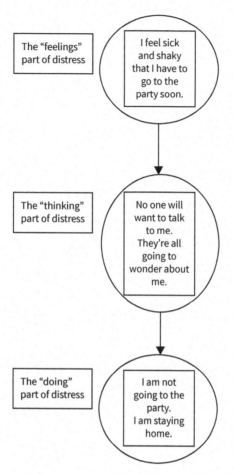

The "feelings" part of distress — I feel sick and shaky that I have to go to the party soon.

The "thinking" part of distress — No one will want to talk to me. They're all going to wonder about me.

The "doing" part of distress — I am not going to the party. I am staying home.

Figure 4.1 Distress diagram (party).

distress about school. Avoiding school might seem like a good short-term thing to do because distress is lowered, but eventually your child has to go to school.

Think about how your child's distress builds in the morning or during the course of a typical school day. What part of the distress starts first? For some older children and adolescents, the feelings part starts first (Figure 4.2). A teenager may wake up and feel nauseous because a big test is scheduled that day. As the stomach problem

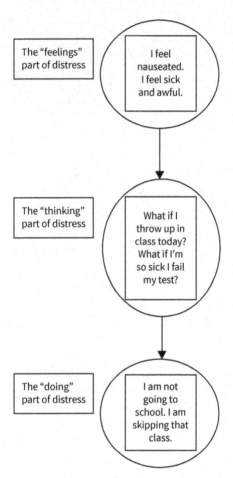

Figure 4.2 Distress diagram (nauseous).

worsens, she may think about terrible things that could happen as a result. She may think, "What if I throw up in class today?" or "What if I'm so sick I fail my test?" As the upsetting feelings and thoughts continue, she may avoid school or skip class (the doing part).

Other teenagers show other patterns of distress (Figure 4.3). Some wake up and *immediately* think about bad things happening: "Oh, no, school today. I know it's going to be awful" (the thinking part). They may become physically unwell, very aroused, or achy as a result

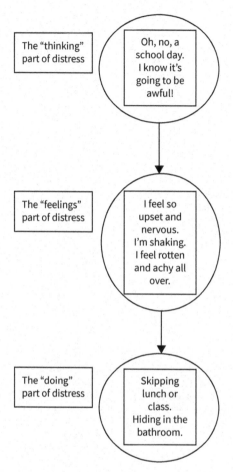

The "thinking" part of distress — Oh, no, a school day. I know it's going to be awful!

The "feelings" part of distress — I feel so upset and nervous. I'm shaking. I feel rotten and achy all over.

The "doing" part of distress — Skipping lunch or class. Hiding in the bathroom.

Figure 4.3 Distress diagram (bathroom).

(the feelings part). At this point, they may ask their parents to allow them to stay home or they may skip lunch or a certain class and hide in the restroom (the doing part).

Other teenagers begin with certain *behaviors* first (Figure 4.4). Some simply refuse to get out of bed. When their parents try to get them out of bed, they may complain about being teased at school or about having to go to physical education class that day. Later, they may feel more queasy or dizzy as they get closer to the school

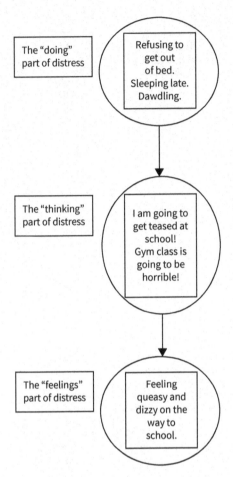

Figure 4.4 Distress diagram (sleep).

building. In this situation, the doing part starts first (refusing to get out of bed), followed by the thinking part (worries about teasing or class), followed by the feelings part (queasy, dizzy).

What pattern of distress best fits your child? In the margins, draw the most common pattern of distress that you see in your child. Feel free to follow the examples given in the figures by drawing circles and arrows and by writing a description of each part. If your child shows different patterns of distress on different days, that's okay. List all of the different patterns of distress that she shows.

Changing the Feeling Part of Distress

Now that you have mapped out your child's pattern of distress, see whether you listed any physical feelings that she may have. If your child has *no* physical feelings of distress, then this section will be less helpful to you. If your child does have some physical feelings of distress, then this section will be more helpful to you.

A reminder: Be sure that any physical feelings or symptoms that your child may have are not caused by a medical condition. The methods in this chapter will be less helpful if your child's symptoms are caused by an illness or medical condition. If you are unsure, then visit your family pediatrician as soon as possible for a medical evaluation.

There are different methods to ease your child's physical feelings of distress. Easing feelings of distress is done by helping children control their arousal and relax. A child cannot be physically tense and relaxed at the same time, so we want to make sure that your child is relaxed instead of tense. I discussed methods of relaxation in detail in Chapter 3, so I invite you to read that chapter (if you have not already done so) to learn about and practice detailed methods of better breathing, muscle relaxation, and general relaxation.

Methods of relaxation are important but many kids who are distressed about social and performance situations at school are more upset by their *thoughts that something bad will happen in these situations.* A main focus of this chapter is to help you help your child change the thinking part of her distress. Let's talk about this next.

Changing the Thinking Part of Distress

If your teenager is distressed about social or performance situations at school, then she likely worries a lot about bad things happening during these situations. As mentioned earlier, some nervousness about social and performance situations is normal because everyone gets a little uptight when meeting people for the first time, speaking in front of others, or singing or playing a musical instrument at a recital. Most of us are able to set aside our worry and do what we have to do. We go on a job interview even though we feel uncomfortable during the evaluation. Other people, however, worry so much about bad things happening that they become very upset and then avoid situations. Your teenager may be so worried about doing poorly in social or performance situations that she is missing school.

What can we do to help fix this? The main goal here is to help your child think more *realistically* in social and performance situations. Notice that I did not say "think more positively." Telling your child to "think happy thoughts," to "not worry," to "try not to think about it," or that she is a "wonderful child" will not work! If your child has worries about bad things happening at school, that's okay. But your child *must also think more realistically* about what is actually happening in situations at school.

Your teenager might worry that "everyone will laugh at me during my oral presentation." Having this thought is okay *as long as* your child takes a step back, thinks about the thought, and comes up with a more realistic thought, such as "Some kids might laugh, but they're jerks, and most kids will just listen to me." In this situation, your teenager is not asked to block the distressing thought or to come up with a happy thought, such as "It will be okay!" *Instead*, she is asked to come up with a *more realistic thought* about what is *most likely to happen* during the oral presentation. When we think more realistically, we understand that the chance of bad things happening is actually small, and we often feel less distressed.

Changing the thinking part of distress is something that you and your child must work on *together*. In addition, for these methods to be effective, the following must apply:

- You and your child *must have* a strong relationship that includes good communication.
- Your child *must be* fairly verbal and willing to discuss her worries in detail.

- In general, your child should be at least 11 years old.
- Your child *must be* doing fairly well in school or would be doing well if she were in school more.
- Your child's level of distress *must be* mild or moderate and *not* severe. Also, she should not be having panic attacks.
- Your child *must have* good social skills, such as the ability to make eye contact with others when speaking, to talk loud enough for others to hear, and to start and maintain conversations.
- Your child *must be* motivated to try to change her thoughts, practice different social and performance situations at school, and eventually go back to school.
- Your child *must not be* faced with legitimate threats at school such as bullies or intimidation.

If any of these is not true, then you may wish to consult a qualified mental health professional (see Chapter 1). This chapter will be more helpful for children who have good social skills, who should be going to school, who are not faced with real threats, and whose thinking part of distress prevents them from speaking to others or performing before others at school.

Distressing Thoughts

What kinds of distressing thoughts do teenagers have in social and performance situations? Distressed teens often make the following mistakes in their thinking:

- They assume that something bad *is happening* when actually it is not. A teenager may assume that others are laughing at her as she enters a classroom when actually they are laughing at some inside joke.
- They assume terrible things *will happen* when terrible things are not likely to happen. A teenager may assume that other kids will

throw food at him during lunchtime when the chances of this happening are actually quite small.

- They assume they know what other people are thinking about them even though they cannot know (*mind reading*). A teenager may assume that others believe she is ugly when she has no real knowledge of this.
- They *jump to conclusions* from just one event or make "mountains out of molehills" by assuming that the consequences of their acts will be extremely bad. A teenager may worry that he is going to fail the entire semester because of a couple of poor test marks.
- They assume they will be *intensely embarrassed*. A teenager may assume she will sing off key in choir, become very embarrassed, and feel so mortified that she can never attend school again.
- They see situations as only *perfect or awful* and not somewhere in between. A teenager may assume that his school day was terrible even though some good things did happen.
- They focus much more on the *negative than the positive* side of things. A teenager who performed at a recital may concentrate on some wrong notes that she played instead of her good overall performance of the musical piece.
- They *blame themselves* for things that are not within their control. A teenager may become upset that two of her friends are arguing and blame herself for not getting more involved.

Do any of these sound familiar to you or your teenager? Are there other thoughts that your child has in social or performance situations that make her very upset? Use the worksheet that is provided (Worksheet 4.1). *In the first column*, ask your child to write all social or performance situations that upset her at school. *In the second column*, ask your child to write her distressing thoughts in these situations. Update these lists once a week as you work with your child. Feel free to photocopy this worksheet or download multiple copies from the companion website (www.oxfordclinicalpsych. com/schoolattendance).

Worksheet 4.1
Social and Performance Situations and Thoughts

Social/performance situations that   *My thoughts in this situation (T)*
bother me (S)

_____   _____

_____   _____

_____   _____

_____   _____

_____   _____

_____   _____

_____   _____

_____   _____

_____   _____

Changing Distressing Thoughts

If your child is going to school for most of the day, then schedule a discussion each evening about distressing thoughts that she had during certain social or performance situations at school that day. If your child is not going to school right now, then work toward a part-time attendance schedule (see next section on the doing part of distress). If your child is not going to school right now, then ask her to describe thoughts she had in the past about social and performance situations at school. If your child cannot come up with any thoughts, then this section will be less helpful.

Once you have a good idea of what distressing thoughts or worries your child has at school, then you can start to help him or her change these thoughts. To first do so, encourage your child to use the acronym *STOP*:

- S: Am I *scared* or nervous about a certain social or performance situation?
- T: What *thoughts* am I having in this situation?
- O: What *other*, more realistic, thoughts can I have?
- P: *Praise* myself for thinking more realistic thoughts (adapted from Silverman & Kurtines, 1996)

Whenever your child is in a social or performance situation that causes her to be distressed, she should practice the STOP method. First, she should recognize what social and performance situations cause her the most distress; this is the *S* part of STOP. When in this social or performance situation, your child should ask herself, "Am I currently *scared* or nervous?" If your child answers yes to this question, then she should think about what distressing, unrealistic, or negative *thoughts* she is having in that situation; this is the *T* part of STOP. Ask your child to keep a written log of her thoughts in these situations so that you can discuss them together.

If your child is having distressing, unrealistic, or negative thoughts in a social or performance situation, then she should think about *other, more realistic thoughts*; this is the *O* part of STOP. We discuss these other thoughts in the next section. Finally, if your child was able to think more realistic thoughts in this situation, then she should silently *praise herself for* doing so; this is the *P* part of STOP. She can say things such as "Good job!" "Great thinking!" or "I am proud of myself."

Have your child practice the STOP method as much as possible whenever she is distressed in a social or performance situation at school. Your child should practice this method so often that it becomes automatic or "second nature." In other words, we want your child to practice developing more realistic thoughts in a given situation and come to realize that the chances of bad things happening are actually low, and that the consequences of most situations are not that bad. Let's talk next about developing more realistic thoughts, the *O* part of STOP.

More Realistic Thoughts

If your child is having distressing thoughts in a social or performance situation at school, then be sure that she lists these thoughts for later discussion. As you and your child discuss these thoughts, *do not be judgmental or critical.* Having distressing thoughts is a normal human experience; we simply have to be sure that distressing thoughts are balanced and eventually replaced by more realistic thoughts. Let's talk in more detail about how this can be done for the different thoughts I listed earlier.

As you and your child discuss distressing thoughts, ask her to keep the following questions in mind as she challenges these thoughts:

> Am I 100% sure that this will happen (or is happening)?
> Can I really know what that person thinks of me?
> What's the worst thing that can really happen?
> Have I ever been in this situation before, and was it really that bad?
> How many times has this terrible thing actually happened?
> Am I the only person that has ever had to deal with this situation?
> So what if I'm not perfect in this situation?
> Is this really my fault?
>
> (Adapted from Kearney & Albano, 2018)

One type of distressing thought occurs when a teenager assumes that terrible things are happening when in fact they are not. A teenager may assume that others are laughing at her as she enters a classroom when actually they are laughing at a joke. If your child has this kind of thought, then encourage her to come up with more realistic thoughts by thinking about what other explanations are more likely. Use the worksheet, STOP method, and questions outlined above.

You: Okay, you wrote down that your *S* today was when you walked into class and that you thought [*T*] the other kids might be laughing at you when you went into class, right?

Your child: Yeah, they were all joking around, and I felt really bad.

You: Okay, so let's talk about the *O* part, some other thoughts you could have. Are you 100% sure that they were laughing at you? Be honest.

Your child: Not 100%, I guess; I don't know.

You: Okay, good. What else might have been going on?

Your child: I don't know.

You: Well, let's think about it. What else could they have been laughing at?

Your child: They're always joking around, saying dumb things. I guess they could have been doing that.

You: Great job coming up with a different thought! Yeah, you're right, maybe they were laughing at something else, because that's what they do?

Your child: Yeah, I guess that could have been happening [then praise (*P*) this new thought].

Another type of distressing thought that many teenagers have is assuming that terrible things will happen. A teenager who has to talk to other kids at school may assume that others will not speak to her. If your child has this kind of thought, then encourage her to come up with more realistic thoughts by thinking about the worst thing that can actually happen and how many times this terrible thing has actually happened. Use the worksheet, STOP method, and questions outlined above.

You: Okay, you wrote down that your *S* today was being nervous about talking to those kids about your homework assignment and that you thought [*T*] they would ignore you, right?

Your child: Yeah, I figured they would just look away.

You: Okay, so let's talk about the *O* part. What was the worst thing that could have happened if they ignored you? What would happen then? Be honest.

Your child: Well, I'd look like an idiot I guess.

You: Okay, good. Even if the worst thing happened, and you felt kind of dumb, what could you do then?

Your child: I'd just ask somebody else.

You: Great! So, even if the worst thing happened, you could handle it, right?

Your child: Yeah, that's true.

You: And how many times have the other kids just completely ignored you?

Your child: Well, it did happen once, but usually people are nice.

You: So . . .

Your child: So I guess that the other kids won't usually ignore me, but if they do, I can just ask somebody else.

You: Great job! [*P*]

Another type of distressing thought that many teenagers have is assuming what others are thinking (mind reading). Teenagers who are nervous in social and performance situations sometimes think they know what others are thinking and that those thoughts must be bad. A teenager playing a musical instrument may assume that audience members think his performance is terrible, so he becomes upset. If your child has this kind of thought, then encourage her to come up with more realistic thoughts by thinking about what other explanations are more likely and whether she really knows what others are thinking. Use the worksheet, STOP method, and questions outlined above.

You: Okay, you wrote down that your *S* today was the recital and that you thought [*T*] the audience thought your performance was awful, right?

Your child: Yeah, I made some mistakes, and I'm sure they thought I couldn't play.

You: Okay, so let's talk about the *O* part. Are you 100% sure that they were thinking that? Can you really know what other people are thinking about you? Be honest.

Your child: No, I was so busy reading the music I couldn't really look at the audience.

You: Okay, good. What else might they have been thinking?

Your child: I don't know, maybe that I made some mistakes?

You: Well, maybe, but you were playing in a full orchestra, right? When someone makes a mistake, can the audience really tell?

Your child: Not really. You can only tell the music is off when everybody is making a whole bunch of mistakes. Maybe they couldn't tell about me.

You: Great job coming up with a different thought! [*P*] Yeah, you're right, maybe they didn't notice your mistakes because you're just one player in the orchestra?

Your child: Yeah, I guess that's right.

Another type of distressing thought is when teenagers jump to conclusions from just one event or make mountains out of molehills. They may assume that the consequences of their actions will be extremely bad. A teenager could assume that she is going to fail a course based on one bad test score. If your child has this kind of thought, then encourage her to come up with more realistic thoughts by thinking about what other explanations are more likely and whether the consequence (failing) is really likely to happen. Use the worksheet, STOP method, and questions outlined above.

You: Okay, you wrote down that your *S* today was that you got a poor grade on your test and that you thought [*T*] you would fail the whole course, right?

Your child: Yeah, I really blew that test. I can't believe it! I know I'm going to fail.

You: Okay, so let's talk about the *O* part. Are you 100% sure you will fail the whole course? What is the worst thing that can happen when you do poorly on just one test? Be honest.

Your child: Well, I might fail—I don't know. Plus, there are lots of quizzes and tests this semester in that course. Plus a ton of homework and other assignments!

You: Right, so . . .

Your child: So I guess doing bad on one test won't kill me. But I can't keep doing bad!

You: Right, that's true, and we'll work on that. I'll help you. But you understand that one bad grade doesn't mean you'll fail the whole semester?

Your child: Yeah, I guess I got carried away [then praise (*P*) the new thoughts].

Another type of distressing thought is when teenagers assume they will be embarrassed and that the embarrassment will be intense. Older children and adolescents worry a lot about being very embarrassed. They may give an oral presentation and feel bad when tripping up their words. The important thing to remember about embarrassment is that it is temporary and manageable! Tell your child that everyone gets embarrassed (give some personal examples), that embarrassment doesn't usually last long, and that your child can handle the embarrassment. Use the worksheet, STOP method, and questions outlined above.

You: Okay, you wrote down that your *S* was giving your oral report and that you thought [*T*] you were embarrassed, right?

Your child: Yeah, I kept tripping over my words and felt stupid. I was *so* embarrassed!

You: Yeah, I can understand that. But let's think about the *O* part. You know, everyone gets embarrassed from time to time. Remember that time I fell off the boat and into the lake with all my clothes on at the family reunion?

Your child: [Laughing] Yeah, who could forget that!

You: I felt pretty embarrassed, but everybody gets embarrassed. Have you ever been embarrassed before?

Your child: Well, yeah, remember the time I fell off the stage during the church play?

You: Yep. And what did you do?

Your child: I just got back on stage and kept going, but I felt terrible.

You: How long did you feel terrible?

Your child: A couple of hours I guess.

You: Right, you felt embarrassed, but it went away and you were able to handle it, right?

Your child: Yeah, I guess so.

You: So . . .

Your child: So I guess feeling embarrassed today will go away, too. I already feel better now than I did at school. And I was able to finish my talk.

You: Great job! [the *P* part]

Another type of distressing thought that many teenagers have is assuming that things are either perfect or awful and not in between. A teenager may come home and sulk that her day was terrible because of a couple of arguments with her friends. She may ignore the fact that the rest of her day went well. Or a child may be upset because he did not get a perfect grade on a test. If your child has this kind of thought, then encourage her to come up with more realistic thoughts by thinking about the entire day. Use the worksheet, STOP method, and questions outlined above.

You: Okay, you wrote down that your *S* was having a terrible day because of the arguments with your friends, and that you thought [*T*] the day was terrible, right?

Your child: Yeah, I just feel so awful about it. I really don't want to go back to school tomorrow.

You: It's okay to feel that way. But let's talk about the *O* part. Was every hour or 100% of the day so terrible?

Your child: Well, no, I got a great grade on my math test and had a lot of fun at lunch with Tamatha and Justine.

You: Great! It sounds like some of the day went well, then.

Your child: Yeah, that's true; most of the day was okay.

You: So what if your day isn't perfect, right? Is any day really perfect, where nothing bad happens?

Your child: Not really. Not in my high school anyway.

You: My day had its ups and downs, too. Everyone's does. If a day isn't perfect, then it's a normal day!

Your child: Yeah, I guess that's right [then praise (*P*) the new thoughts].

My Child Is a Perfectionist!

Some children have trouble going to school because they are afraid of making mistakes. These kids may be perfectionistic: This means that they want everything to be perfect and worry a lot about the consequences of doing something wrong or handing in an assignment that might have an error. Other perfectionists cannot complete written work because they are constantly checking and rechecking their paper. As a result, some of these kids become very distressed and may even fail their classes because nothing is being handed in! Worse yet, some refuse to go to school.

If your child is perfectionistic, then concentrate on the thinking part of distress. Be sure your child understands that the consequences of handing in a paper with a couple of misspellings or a test with a couple of errors are not dire—a child will not fail class or be yelled at or judged harshly if a couple of mistakes are made. *In addition, be sure that you are not aggravating your child's perfectionism.* Children who are perfectionistic may have parents who are perfectionistic; as a result, children may feel a lot of pressure to do well and actually fear making mistakes. Tell your child that mistakes are normal, and that you will not be angry if minor mistakes are made.

Another recommendation involves the doing part of perfectionism. I sometimes ask perfectionistic children to deliberately hand in work that has a couple of mistakes. As they do so, I ask them to practice relaxation, think realistically, and see that the consequences of the mistakes are not that bad. I stress that work needs to be handed in on time, and that they must attend school. If this means a couple of minor mistakes, that is fine.

Another type of distressing thought that many teenagers have is fo-cusing much more on the negative than the positive. Teenagers who are nervous about going back to school after some absence may worry about questions and comments that others may make about their absence. In addition, they may ignore the positive things that might happen. If your child has this kind of thought, then encourage her to come up with more realistic thoughts by thinking about positives as well as negatives. Use the worksheet, STOP method, and questions outlined above.

You: Okay, you wrote down that your *S* is having to go back to school tomorrow, and that you thought [*T*] a lot of people are going to bother you with questions, right?

Your child: Yeah, everybody's going to ask me where I was and every-thing. I just don't want to be bothered! Can't I stay home just one more day?

You: No, you're going to school tomorrow. Let's talk about the *O* part. What else do you think everyone will say to you?

Your child: Some people will be glad I'm back. Justin called earlier and said, "See you tomorrow!"

You: Great! So you might get some looks and stares, and some people might wonder where you were, but other people will welcome you back, right?

(For more information on what children can say to others when they go back to school, see Chapter 6).

Your child: Yeah, I think so. And my teachers won't say anything.

You: And do you think you'll be bothered with questions all day long?

Your child: No, probably just the morning, and I know what I can say.

You: Great! [the *P* part]

Another type of distressing thought that many teenagers have is blaming themselves for things that are beyond their control. A teenager may blame herself for conflict between two of her friends. If your child has this kind of thought, then encourage her to come up with more realistic thoughts by thinking about what other explanations are more likely and whether she could really control what happened. Use the worksheet, STOP method, and questions outlined above.

You: Okay, you wrote down that your *S* was your two friends arguing, and that you thought [*T*] you were upset and down on yourself, right?

Your child: Yeah, they broke up and won't speak to each other. I feel so bad.

You: Why?

Your child: Because maybe I could have talked to them more.

You: Okay, let's think about the *O* part. Is this really your fault? What else might have caused them to break up?

Your child: Well, they're always arguing, and Dominic even hung out with another girl!

You: Those sound like pretty good reasons for a breakup, don't they?

Your child: Yeah, I guess so. But I still feel bad.

You: Yes, it's okay for you to feel bad for your friends, as long as you understand that sometimes people don't get along, and that's not always our fault, right?

Your child: Yeah, that's true. Maybe I can just keep being their friend [then praise (*P*) the new thoughts].

Practicing the STOP Method

If your child has a lot of distressing thoughts about social and performance situations at school, then talk to her *each day* about these thoughts and help her change the thoughts to more realistic ones. Have your child use the worksheet, practice the STOP method, and draw on the questions listed here to take a step back, look at distressing thoughts, and come up with more realistic thoughts. With practice, your child should be able to think more realistically and discover that bad things are not likely to happen, and even if they do, that she is likely able to handle whatever does happen.

Changing the Doing Part of Distress

Another important goal of this chapter is changing the doing part of distress. Your child may be (a) missing most of the school day or (b) having trouble going to certain classes or feeling distressed in different social or performance situations at school. Let's talk about these separately.

Missing Most of the School Day

If your child is missing most or all of the school day, then the first step toward full-time school attendance should be small. Ask your child what time of day is easiest for her to go to school. Teenagers often say that they would go to school as long as they didn't have to attend one or two key classes, such as physical education or English class. So I tell them, Go to school except for physical education and English class! Find out what time of day your child is willing to go to school and use that as a starting point. Then you and she can gradually increase the amount of time spent in school.

If your child is missing most or all of the school day, then pursuing a part-time schedule at first is a good idea. As mentioned in Chapter 3, the first step in a part-time schedule can involve one of the following:

- Your child goes to school in the morning and is then allowed to come home within an hour (then gradually work forward by adding more time).
- Your child goes to school at 2 p.m. and is then allowed to come home when school normally ends, say at 3:10 p.m. (then gradually work backward by adding more time).
- Your child goes to school only for lunch and is then allowed to come home afterward (then gradually add more school time before and after lunch).
- Your child goes to school only for her favorite class or time of day (then gradually add more classes or school time).

- Your child attends a school room other than his classroom, such as the school library, school counselor or nurse's office, or main lobby (then gradually add more classroom time).

I covered these steps at length in Chapter 3, so I will not repeat myself here. If your child is missing most of the school day, then I invite you to read Chapter 3 and, in particular, the section on changing the doing part of distress. This section will give you detailed ideas about how to set up a part-time attendance schedule that will eventually lead to full-time attendance. Be sure your child practices changing the feeling and thinking parts of distress even during the part-time school schedule. If your child does go to school for most of the day but has trouble skipping one or two classes or being in different social or performance situations at school, then read the next section.

Trouble in Social and Performance Situations at School

If your child is skipping a key class or two, such as physical education class, or goes to school but has a lot of distress about social or performance situations when there, then this section is for you. If your child is skipping one or two classes, be sure that she continues to go to school for the other classes. In addition, arrange with school officials some place that your child can go, other than hiding somewhere, during the skipped classes. If your child will not go to physical education class, arrange so that she can spend the time (for now) in the school library or counselor's office. That way she is at least supervised and you can monitor how much time she spent in class. Gradually more time in physical education class can be scheduled later.

Many kids are nervous about tests and have trouble going to classes when tests are scheduled. In this case, get sample tests from different teachers that your child can practice at school or home. As your child is practicing these tests, time the tests just as they would be timed in school. In addition, have your child practice methods to relax and change distressing thoughts described in this chapter. Talk to your child about what thoughts she may be having during the first 5 minutes of the sample test. Many teenagers worry about failing or "freezing up." If this is the case, then help your child physically relax and think realistically using questions such as "Are you 100% sure you will fail or freeze?" "What is the worst thing that could happen if you did fail or freeze?" and "Are you the only person who is nervous about taking this test?"

Physical Education Class

One of the toughest classes for many teenagers to attend is physical education. Many teens do not like physical education because they have to change clothes or shower before others, perform athletically before others, and risk being teased, ridiculed, embarrassed, or picked last for a team. As a result, some of them skip physical education class or do not participate very much during the class.

If this applies to your child, then work with her on the methods described in this chapter. Be sure that your child is relaxed and help change distressing thoughts she may have during physical education class. If your child is not participating much in this class, then work on ways that she can talk to others and get more involved with the sports that are being conducted. If your child is teased or ridiculed or always picked last for a team, then talk to the physical education teacher to see how this might be resolved. Perhaps your child can be chosen occasionally to pick a team or a lottery system could be set up where teams are chosen randomly. If your child is embarrassed about how she performs at a sport, then practice the sport with her.

A related problem involves not wanting to undress or shower in the locker room. Do not allow your child to avoid this or to get dressed in a private location. Instead, ask your child to be as prepared as possible with his gear. This means bringing all necessary clothes and getting changed for class as efficiently as possible. Encourage your child to speak to others in the locker room and during physical education class so his focus is on making eye contact and starting and joining conversations and not on worry about being watched or judged.

As your child practices sample tests and becomes better at them, arrange with your child's school counselor and teachers to begin practice tests in the classroom. These can involve tests that are done after school or during a time of day when other people are not around. The tests may or may not count toward your child's actual grade, but the important thing is that your child is practicing the tests and taking them with less distress. As your child becomes better at taking these tests, she can start taking them during regularly scheduled classes. *Continue to rate your child's distress using the worksheet provided in* Chapter 2 *so you can see whether progress is being made.*

The same can be done for other situations that teenagers sometimes avoid, the following for example:

- Have your child practice oral presentations or write on a board at home or in an empty classroom before doing so in a full classroom setting.
- Have your child practice playing a musical instrument before a small group of people such as relatives, friends, or immediate family members before doing so in front of larger audiences.
- Have your child practice asking and answering questions with a teacher when no one is around before doing so in class.
- Have your child practice other performances that make her nervous such as driving, eating in a cafeteria, using public restrooms, undressing and showering with people nearby, and walking into school or class.

As your child practices these situations, help her relax and change distressing thoughts to more realistic ones. Continue to rate your child's level of distress in these situations. Many kids need a lot of practice in these situations before they feel completely comfortable, so be patient and persistent. In addition, reward your child for practicing these different tasks.

What about social situations at school? As mentioned earlier, many teens are shy and have trouble speaking to other kids at school. If this is so for your child, then she needs to practice different kinds of social situations, such as the following:

- Walking up to others to ask a question
- Starting a conversation in a relaxed area such as the cafeteria, bus, playground, or extracurricular activity
- Asking someone to stop doing something annoying
- Joining a group of kids who are already doing something together
- Calling a classmate to get a homework assignment
- Asking and answering questions in class

Extracurricular Activities

Extracurricular activities are school-related clubs, groups, teams, and other peer gatherings where kids share a common interest and can make new friends. Extracurricular activities can have a strong impact on school attendance. Many kids have trouble going to school because they feel isolated, lonely, and "on the outside looking in." They may be in a racial minority, new to a school, or shy in general. As a result, they sometimes do not feel motivated to go to class. If this applies to your child, then one way to change this is to get her more involved in extracurricular activities so she can develop friends who might share her classes.

As a first step, get a list of available extracurricular activities from your child's school counselor or website. Then sit down and talk to your child about which activities interest her the most. Do not let your child get away with saying "none of these." Some activities will be more liked than others, and your child can try those first. I recommend that your child try at least three activities for a month. That way, even if one or two don't work out, another is still available. Also, encourage your child to make friends with peers in these groups. Encourage her to call or text these other kids, make plans to see a movie, or invite them over.

On the other hand, be careful not to overload your child with too many extracurricular activities. Some teens have difficulty attending school because they are so overwhelmed with schoolwork, a part-time job, a sports team, and several other activities. If this is the case, then ask your child where some time might be saved and then allow her to gradually withdraw from some commitments.

Like performance situations, these social situations can be practiced outside of school in comfortable places like home or in a church group. You can even act out different situations for your child such as pretending to be the teacher as your child asks a question. As your child does this, let her know what could be done a little differently to be more effective. Your child may have to speak more clearly, make better eye contact, and pause a little before responding.

A reminder: If your child has a great deal of trouble with these situations, then seeking the help of a qualified mental health professional may be necessary (see Chapter 1). The recommendations made in this chapter are for teenagers who have some, *but not severe*, trouble attending school due to distress about social or performance situations there. In addition, the methods described here must be done with the cooperation of school officials. Solving school attendance problems takes the effort of everyone working together—you, your child, and your child's school officials.

Do's and Don'ts!

I know that I have given you a lot of information in this chapter. Here is a list of some do and don't reminders.

Do:

- Help your child understand the different parts of distress: the physical feelings, thinking, and doing parts of distress.
- Think about how these different parts of distress occur in your child.
- Teach your child better breathing by using deep, slow, diaphragmatic breathing.
- Teach your child to relax her muscles using the tense-and-release method.
- Encourage your child to relax in general and give her feedback about doing so.

- Work each evening with your child to help her think more realistically in social and performance situations.
- Work with your child to practice social and performance situations that he or she has difficulty with.
- Work closely with school officials.
- Set up a part-time school attendance schedule if necessary.
- Seek support from others.
- Be consistent and use these methods every day.

Don't:
- Argue, yell, lecture, criticize, negotiate, beg, or bribe your child to go to school.
- Ignore your child's distress.
- Use statements such as "Don't worry," "Think happy thoughts," "There's nothing to be afraid of," "You're not really upset," or "You're faking it."
- Allow your child to come home early or do fun things during school hours.

Other Skills

Anxious middle/high school teenagers sometimes lose ability in certain skills if they have missed a lengthy time at school. These skills can include asserting oneself in different situations, inviting others to social events, managing conflict with others, interacting with people in public spaces, speaking with unknown authority figures, managing negative feedback or comments from others, handling difficult or unpredictable situations, or solving problems independently. If this is the case for your child, then work with school officials to improve these skills or seek consultation from a qualified mental health professional (see Chapter 1). Some anxious teenagers also respond well to mindfulness techniques under the supervision of a qualified mental health professional.

Final Comments

Having a child who is distressed about school and who is missing school can be very upsetting, but the problem is fixable! Easing a child's distress about social and performance situations demands a lot of practice. Keep practicing those situations that give your child difficulty until she can do them well. Also, be patient, seek support from others in your life, and cooperate with school officials who can help. You can do it!

5

The Attention-Seeking Elementary School Child

Sam is an 8-year-old boy who has problems attending school because he would much rather be with his mother at home. Sam often refuses to go to school in the morning, although his mom can sometimes get him to go into the school building. Sam says he likes school but often misses his mother. Whenever he is at school, Sam tries to call his mother and has even run out of the school building twice to try to go home. Lately, Sam's mom has been eating lunch with her son in the school cafeteria to get him to go to school.

This chapter will be *more helpful* to you if your child matches Sam's situation or if one of the following is true:

- Your child is refusing school *only* to get attention from you or significant others.
- Your child wants you to attend school with him.
- Your family's morning routine is chaotic.
- Your child is having trouble attending school mostly in the mornings.
- Your child is exaggerating physical complaints (stomachaches, headaches) to try to stay out of school.
- Your child has trouble separating from you or significant others.

This chapter will be *less helpful* to you if one of the following is true:

- Your child is refusing school *only* because he is very distressed about something related to school (see Chapter 3).
- Your child is refusing school *only* because he is very distressed about social or performance situations at school (see Chapter 4).
- Your child is refusing school *only* to do fun activities outside of school during school hours (see Chapter 6).

In Chapter 2 we discussed different reasons why children have trouble going to school. One reason is that some children like Sam seek a lot of attention from one or both parents and are defiant about going to school because they would rather stay home. Sam often resisted going to school in the morning because he wanted to spend the day helping his mom around the home or going with her to her part-time job. He was not upset about school but insisted that his mom be at school during part of the day.

Children who refuse school for attention are often younger and may have temper tantrums in the morning, say they want to stay home from school or have a parent go to school with them, and show stubborn, willful, manipulative, or guilt-inducing behavior to try to stay home. If these children do go to school, then they may constantly call or text their parents during the day, persistently ask the same questions over and over, and even run away from the school building to go home. Many of these children are *not particularly distressed* about school. If you feel that your child *is* distressed about school, then read Chapters 3 and 4.

To change your child's attention-seeking behavior and improve his school attendance, I concentrate on the following:

- Setting up a regular morning routine
- Paying attention to appropriate behaviors and ignoring inappropriate behaviors
- Setting up formal rewards for going to school without behavior problems

- Setting up formal disincentives for refusing school with behavior problems
- Changing what you say to your child
- Handling excessive calls, texts, and questions
- Dealing with a child who runs away from the school building
- Physically bringing a child to attend school under certain circumstances

Why Am I Doing This?

If your child resembles Sam, then he has a lot of control over your family's morning routine. He may be acting a certain way, and everyone else in the family is *reacting* to what he does in the morning. You may be expecting your child to have a temper tantrum and trying to do whatever you can to prevent it, like allowing him to play video games instead of getting a backpack together for school.

You may also be "working with" your child to try to get him to go to school. You may be yelling, lecturing, negotiating, bribing, or constantly nagging your child to go to school. You may be trying to comfort his minor physical complaints or you may keep responding to his constant statements and questions about wanting to stay home. In the meantime, he is still resisting going to school or is missing school! You are *reacting* to what your child is doing and, in doing so, giving him a lot of attention that reinforces his school refusal behaviors (Figure 5.1). I call this "dancing to the child's tune." What ways do you think you might be reacting to your child's behavior or doing extra work to help him out in the morning?

We have to change this. Your child should dance *to your* tune (Figure 5.2). In other words, we have to set up the morning so that your child is responding *to your* rules and to *what you* say and not the other way around. To do this, we have to set up a clear and predictable morning routine that your child is expected to follow *each school day*. If he follows this routine, then good things (rewards)

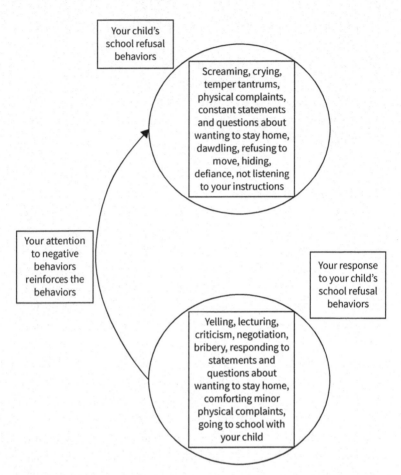

Figure 5.1 Responding to your child's school refusal behavior ("dancing to his tune").

will happen. If he does not follow this routine, then less-than-good things (disincentives) will happen. In this way, your child will be responding to rules and consequences that *you* are putting in place. You are the boss!

Getting your child to respond to your directions also means giving your child commands that are short and to the point. I am sure you are tired of lengthy arguments, reassurances, and promises to get your child to go to school. I will help you make *simple commands* to

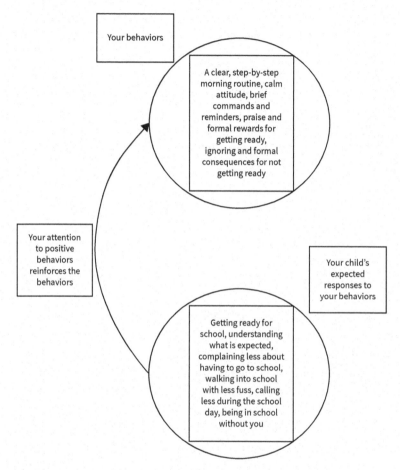

Figure 5.2 Responding to your rules and statements ("dancing to your tune").

your child that he clearly understands and must comply with. Again, if he does comply with these commands, then good things (rewards) will happen. If he does not comply with these commands, then less-than-good things (disincentives) will happen. In this way, your child will be responding to *your* statements.

Getting your child to respond to your directions also means setting *boundaries* on his behavior. I discuss what behaviors to ignore and what behaviors to attend to in the morning, what physical symptoms should allow a child to stay home from school, what to say to a child who asks the same questions over and over, how to handle frequent calls or texts from a child during the day, when to (and not to) go to school with a child, and what to do if a child runs away from the school building. I also cover the topic of physically bringing a child to school.

All of these recommendations require a lot of effort on your part. The methods in this chapter will be helpful *only* if you and/or your spouse/partner:

- Have the *will and the ability* to carry out the methods
- Support each other
- Are confident that your child is refusing school *only* for attention
- Are working closely with school officials
- Can commit to doing the methods consistently and permanently

If you feel a little hesitant or guilty about doing some of the methods in this chapter, that is normal. If you feel very hesitant or guilty, then you must resolve these feelings first. Discuss whatever plan you develop with adult family members and school officials. Most importantly, keep in mind that the methods in this chapter are designed to improve your family's quality of life and your child's quality of life. Your family's quality of life will improve as the morning becomes easier and less tense. Your child's quality of life will improve as he more easily attends school and receives a good education. In the long run, everybody wins!

Setting Up a Regular Morning Routine

If you have a child who is refusing school for attention, or if you have a very chaotic morning routine before school starts, then *the first thing* we have to do is set up a *structured morning routine*. Many parents say that weekday mornings are their most stressful and difficult times of their week, especially when their child is complaining of physical symptoms and constantly asking to stay home. Many parents say their morning routine is rushed, disorganized, and hectic. Part of the reason for this is that a child is dawdling, refusing to move, or having a temper tantrum to try to stay home from school.

We have to change this. *Your first step* is to sit down this evening to plan the morning routine in peace and quiet. All adults in the home must be in on this plan! *Your second step* is to prepare a morning routine that will be the same each morning. Although different things come up each day, try to keep the same schedule each weekday morning. When a child knows what is expected of him each day and what consequences (rewards and disincentives) will follow, then there is less need for constant explaining from parents and arguing among family members.

I recommend that your child rise from bed about 120 minutes before the beginning of school. If your child is expected to enter the school building at 8:50 a.m., then he should be out of bed by 6:50 a.m. This is the example I am using here, but you will have to use whatever times apply most to you. In addition, I am assuming you have a short drive of no more than 10 minutes to your child's school (or your child's bus ride is no more than 10 minutes long). If the commute is longer, then budget for this extra time by having your child get up even earlier.

If your child is expected to rise at, say 6:50 a.m., then an alarm (which may be you) should go off at 6:30, 6:40, and 6:48 a.m. Your child should awake at 6:30, again at 6:40, and again at 6:48 and then be expected to arise from bed at 6:50 a.m. If he does not rise from bed, then you will need to help him do so. You can also remind him that some consequence (reward or disincentive) will follow if he gets out of bed or fails to get out of bed on time (see further section).

The next step in planning the morning routine is to list the preparations that your child is expected to do to get ready for school. These preparations should be listed in the order *that you want*, and each should be given a certain number of minutes to complete. For example, here is a possible scenario:

6:50 a.m.	Rise from bed
6:50–7 a.m.	Go to the bathroom and wash (10 minutes)
7–7:20 a.m.	Eat breakfast (which should be ready by 7 or whenever breakfast time starts) (20 minutes)
7:20–7:30 a.m.	Brush teeth in bathroom and wash as needed (10 minutes)
7:30–7:50 a.m.	Dress and accessorize for school (20 minutes)
7:50–8 a.m.	Make final preparation for school such as putting on a jacket or getting backpack ready (10 minutes)
8–8:20 a.m.	Extra time (if child is ready, provide some reward at this time; if child is not ready, he can use this time to finish) (20 minutes) and final goodbyes.
8:20–8:40 a.m.	Commute to school (20 minutes)
8:40–8:50 a.m.	Child enters school (10 minutes)

Give your child more time than is needed to complete each step. Give your child plenty of time to complete each step *and then add 5 minutes.* If you feel your son can easily dress for school in 10 minutes but often needs 15 minutes because of dawdling, then give him 20 minutes to finish dressing. If your morning routine is flexible like this, then problems such as temper tantrums or dawdling will have less effect. If your child took 13 minutes instead of 10 minutes to go to the bathroom and wash, then this places some pressure but not a lot of pressure on the next step because extra time for the next step is already built in. In this way, your morning routine is not as rushed because plenty of time is provided for each step.

Build into your morning routine a "buffer zone" of extra time. In the routine listed above, "extra time" takes place from 8 to 8:20 a.m. If your son completed all of the morning routine steps and is ready by this time, then some reward (see further section) should be given. He could be allowed to watch a video or read a book. If your child has *not* completed all of the morning routine steps by this time, then the extra time can be used to make sure everything is ready. If your son dawdled and finally got everything ready by 8:15 a.m., then you are still on schedule for bringing him to school. However, this dawdling will need to be linked to a consequence that evening (see further section).

The routine provided here is only an example. You must develop your own routine that is best for you. You may have other children to consider. Or you may prefer a different routine or other step, such as your child taking a shower. Or one adult in the home might have to leave for work in the middle of your child's morning routine, so extra time for each step after that person leaves needs to be budgeted. If your spouse/partner leaves for work *before or during* your child's morning routine, then be sure to budget a lot of extra time for each step. To develop your morning routine, use the worksheet that is provided (Worksheet 5.1). Because your morning routine may change slightly from week to week, feel free to photocopy this worksheet or download multiple copies from the companion website (www.oxfordclinicalpsych.com/schoolattendance).

After you create the morning routine, share it with everyone in the home, including all children and especially the child who is having trouble attending school. You may ask for input but do not negotiate the morning routine with your child. *You are setting up a home rule that must be obeyed.*

After the morning routine has been finalized, try it for a couple of days. Do this to see what needs tweaking. You may find that one particular step needs more time, so the morning routine can be changed slightly to accommodate this. After a couple of days of tweaking, your morning routine should be set.

A clear and regular morning routine is the foundation for the other methods discussed in this chapter. All of the other things I ask you to practice will be much easier if the morning routine is set and everyone knows what is expected. Again, this routine must be practiced consistently each school morning! No exceptions unless some emergency arises! *If you feel you cannot manage the morning routine by yourself, then you must find someone to help you.* Someone could help get the other kids to school as you focus on your child with school attendance problems.

Worksheet 5.1
Our Morning Routine

What I Want My Child to Do

Time to Complete This Step
(e.g., 7–7:20 a.m.)

_____   _____

_____   _____

_____   _____

_____   _____

_____   _____

_____   _____

_____   _____

_____   _____

_____   _____

Returning to School After a Break or Holiday

Some kids have a tough time going back to school after a break or holiday. That's understandable: With 1 or 2 weeks off, it's easy to sleep in, play video games, be with friends, and stay up later at night. When it's time to go back to school, some children naturally have trouble readjusting to a weekday schedule or they become distressed about what will happen once they are back at school.

If this applies to your child, then I recommend starting the "morning school routine" a few days before the onset of school. If your child is off for winter break and has to return to school on January 4, then practice the morning routine as if your child were going to school. Do this for at least a couple of days before the first day back. That way, your child's sleep schedule can get back to normal, and the rush to get ready in the morning can be avoided. If your child is nervous about going back to school, then talk to him about his concerns and practice the methods described in this chapter. In addition, plan something fun for you and your child to do on the evening after that first day back.

If you think your child might have trouble returning to school following the summer break, then restart the morning routine at least a week before school starts. Also, involve your child in various social activities during the summer to help him develop friendships, build social skills, and become more confident in social and performance situations. Camps, sleepovers, games, birthday parties, and family get-togethers are helpful in this regard. Limit the use of electronic devices—instead, celebrate summer together!

Paying Attention to Appropriate Behaviors and Ignoring Inappropriate Behaviors

If your child is like Sam, then he probably receives a lot of attention for refusing to go to school. This is understandable. We as parents sometimes find ourselves lecturing, yelling, cajoling, and begging our children to go to school. When this happens occasionally, it is not too bad. When this happens almost every day, however, it becomes a problem that we must solve.

You may find that you are currently giving your child a lot of attention, even negative attention, for behaviors such as dawdling, refusing to move, physical complaints, or crying. You may feel frustrated when your child will not go to school and naturally turn that frustration into anger. This has not worked, and we have to try a different way.

During the morning routine and as you bring your child to school, *pay attention to appropriate behaviors* such as completing each step of the morning routine and getting on the bus or into the car without a problem. If your child responds well to the morning routine and the other suggestions in this chapter, then be sure to let him know you are happy. Remember that we are talking about a child who likes attention from you. Catch your child being good and praise him for doing what you like.

When your child does something in the morning that you like, such as getting dressed on time, smile, verbally praise, or hug your child as he completes the morning tasks. Tell your child, "I like the way you are dressing yourself" or "Great job eating your breakfast!" Do not take any positive behavior for granted—*reward your child often when he is doing even minor things that help the process of going to school.* Of course, you cannot reward every little thing your child does during the morning but sprinkle your attention throughout the morning so your child feels rewarded and motivated to get ready for school.

As much as possible, also try to ignore *inappropriate behaviors* such as dawdling, crying, minor physical complaints, and temper tantrums. I know this can be hard to do. The idea is to let your child know that he has to prepare for school despite any problems he has in doing so. You should draw your attention away from behaviors that we do not want to see. In that way, the behaviors will not be rewarded and they should lessen. Ignoring inappropriate behaviors will take some work on your part because it may not be what you are used to doing. You must practice this! Have other people help you with this by reminding you when you should be ignoring a certain behavior.

What about physical complaints? We certainly do not want to ignore real symptoms, but I recommend that a child go to school *except* when there is

- A temperature of 100 degrees Fahrenheit or more
- Frequent vomiting
- Bleeding

- Lice
- Severe diarrhea
- Severe flu-like symptoms
- Another severe medical condition or pain

If your child has these problems, then visit your pediatrician (see Chapter 3 for more information on physical complaints). Even under some of these circumstances, some children can go to school. Your child may have limited diarrhea in the morning before school but not when going to school or when at school. In this case, he can still be expected to go to school. A good idea is to assume that your child is going to school and that only unusual circumstances such as high temperature will allow you to consider letting a child stay home from school. Try to build this expectation in *your child*: Yes, you are going to school today!

Setting Up Formal Rewards for Going to School

Paying attention to good morning behaviors is very important, and there is even more you can do to encourage your child to prepare for and go to school—*formal rewards*. Formal rewards include things a child can touch and see such as access to electronic devices or playing a game. Formal rewards can be given in the morning *and* the evening. If your child completes the morning routine without any problems, then use the morning "buffer time" to give formal rewards. A child who is ready by 8 a.m. and who does not have to leave the home until 8:30 a.m. can be allowed to play, read, or do some fun (though brief) activity with you. You should be ready by this time as well (say, 8) so that you can give your child formal rewards as they are needed.

If your child prepares for school, leaves home, and goes to school without any problems such as temper tantrums, then be sure to provide some reward during the evening. Again, because these children like attention, good rewards include staying up a little later, doing fun activities with a parent, reading stories together, running errands together, or walking the dog together. Remind your child why he is getting this reward—that going to school without a problem means good things! *Also, be sure to give some reward, even a little one, every day your child goes to school without a problem.*

Setting Up Formal Disincentives for Refusing to Go to School

What happens if your child *does have trouble* getting through the morning routine and going to school? If this is the case, then the first thing you should check is whether the morning routine you have set up is too difficult for your child. If you feel this might be so, then tweak the routine so that your child has plenty of time to complete each step.

The second thing you should do is decide which of your child's morning behaviors are most challenging: What *specifically* does your child do in the morning that is most difficult for you? Many parents answer this question by giving general statements such as "not going to school" or "goofing around." Instead, think about *very specific behavior problems* that your child shows in the morning. Some of these behaviors may come from the worksheet regarding morning problems (see Chapter 2 and Worksheet 2.4). Continue to keep a checklist of these behaviors each day and pick which ones seem most challenging.

Start by picking *two behavior problems* that are most challenging for you. Focus on providing consequences for these two behavior problems first. Once they lessen, then other behavior problems can be given a consequence as well. These behavior problems will likely include:

- Not finishing or not even trying the morning routine (including a lot of dawdling)
- Temper tantrums that involve crying, screaming, or kicking
- Refusing to move, such as not leaving bed, the home, or the car
- Refusing to enter the school building
- Running away from home or the school building

All of these morning behavior problems, and others that you may have listed, interfere with your child's ability to go to school on time. Therefore, the behaviors *must be linked to a disincentive*. The purpose of a disincentive is not to hurt a child or vent a parent's anger but rather to *clearly teach a child* which behaviors are expected and rewarded and which behaviors are unacceptable. When done correctly and with rewards for good behavior, disincentives can be an effective tool for shaping a child's behavior. Remember, we are setting up a system where your child dances to *your* tune!

Many parents say they do not like giving a disincentive to their child for problems going to school. This is understandable. Disincentives can sometimes be a hard and unpleasant thing to do. However, we are talking about a child who *should be going to school and who is not distressed about* school. If your son refused to pick up his jacket after you told him to do so, you would find this unacceptable. Refusing school for attention is the same thing. Your child should be listening to what you say about going to school but is not. We have to change this.

As with rewards, disincentives can occur in the morning and evening. Giving a disincentive in the morning as he is refusing to get ready can be a little tricky. Sometimes a disincentive for an attention-seeking child can be as simple as ignoring a temper tantrum or screaming fit (see previous section). Try to ignore these kinds of acting-out (disruptive) behaviors in the morning as much as possible. Continue with your routine as if going to school and work is expected.

If your child knows that acting-out (disruptive) behaviors such as tantrums will not get any attention, then he is less likely to continue the behaviors. If you are ignoring this kind of behavior, then set a timer nearby to let your child know how many minutes he has left to complete a certain step in the morning routine, such as getting dressed. That way you are giving your child feedback about what he needs to do, but you are not giving extra verbal attention to the tantrum or screaming.

A disincentive in the morning can also involve loss of "free time." If your son is not ready by 8 a.m., then he will have to use his extra "buffer time" you built into your morning routine to finish getting ready. If he has a temper tantrum, then you can restrict the kinds of activities he does during this free time. You could tell him that he loses access to electronic devices during the free time because he was screaming and saying, "No!" If he is ready by 8 despite the screaming fit, then he may lose access to electronic devices but still be allowed some other activity such as reading.

Disincentives for inappropriate behavior should also occur in the evening. *My rule of thumb is that a disincentive should last double the number of minutes that a child was disruptive in the morning.* If a child's temper tantrum lasted 10 minutes in the morning, then the evening disincentive should last 20 minutes. If a child completed the morning routine but then refused to enter the school building for 15 minutes, then the evening disincentive should last 30 minutes. If a child was late finishing the morning routine by 7 minutes, then the evening disincentive should last 14 minutes. These disincentives would be in addition to any given in the morning.

Disincentives should involve some loss of attention from you. Examples include having to go to bed early, losing an activity with a parent, and having to stay in one's room without electronics. I do not recommend physical punishment because loss of attention is usually more effective with these younger children. Linking school absences to physical punishment does not improve the situation and can make it worse.

If your child misses many of the steps in the morning routine or has many problems entering school, then much of the evening will serve as disincentive time. "Yikes," you might say! But this sounds worse than it is. What I mean is that a child who was very disruptive in the morning before school should spend the evening without privileges such as video games, computer time, or playing with friends. Instead, your child could complete chores around the home, do schoolwork, and go to bed early. In addition, tell your child that tomorrow is a new day and that better things will happen if he goes to school without a problem.

Some parents say that their child has built up a huge amount of minutes that are owed in disincentives. A child may have completely refused to go to school for a week and now owes his parents many hours of disincentive time. If this is the case, then allow your child to do something on the weekend as "community service" to clean the slate. Ask your child to clean the garage, weed the yard, or wash the windows (all with your help and supervision) for a full morning. Once your child has done this, tell him the slate is now clean and that you expect him to go to school on Monday.

Do not threaten extreme disincentives! Some parents believe that one large disincentive will motivate a child to go to school, but this does not work in the long run. Some parents threaten to cancel a child's birthday party, take away social activities for a month, or not celebrate a major holiday. There are some big problems with this. First, you cannot do extreme disincentives every day, and many kids do refuse school daily. Second, most parents back off their threats to do something this drastic, which hurts their credibility: Why would a child listen to such threats if they are never carried out? Besides, could you or would you really want to carry out these kinds of disincentives?

The best disincentives for refusing school are those that are basic and those that are done daily and consistently. Remember that your child likes attention from you, so the best disincentives will involve your disappointment and lack of attention. Do not shun your child but do make it clear that you expect him to make better choices and to go to school. *And do not forget to praise and give rewards for positive behaviors such as completing the morning routine!* Rewards *and* disincentives, not either alone, will work best for school attendance problems.

Changing What You Say to Your Child

At this point you have a lot to do: You must create and manage the morning routine and give rewards and disincentives when needed. However, I must ask you to work on another task as well. This has to do with what you say to your child in the morning and how you say it: speaking in short, clear sentences and using a tone of voice that is calm and matter-of-fact.

When your child refuses to go to school, there is always the temptation to lecture your way out of the situation. Some parents go on and on with their child about how his behavior is hurting them or about how bad he is being. Other parents criticize their children or yell at them for not going to school. Still other parents make the mistake of bargaining with their children, promising them wonderful things if they just go to school! Unfortunately, these practices do not work.

We have to do something else. When you speak to your child in the morning, or tell him something to do (a command), keep the following in mind:

- Tell your child *exactly* what you want him to do.
- Give short, direct commands.
- Make direct eye contact when speaking to your child or giving him a command.
- Make sure your child can actually do what you are asking.
- Do the task with your child.
- Reward good listening.

Let's talk about these in detail. When you want your child to do something, *be very specific!* Parents often tell their children to "clean their room" or "get ready for school," but these statements are unclear. Your idea of a clean room and your child's idea of a clean room may be very different! Try more specific statements such as "pick up your clothes from the floor within 5 minutes" and "put your notebooks in your backpack right now." An advantage of saying something like this is that your child understands what you want, and it will be easy for you to check to see that it was done. Being specific in your commands will also make it easy for you to know if a reward or disincentive is needed. If your son did not put his notebooks into his backpack, then it's clear he didn't listen to you and that a consequence may be needed.

When giving a command to your child, be *very brief* in what you say. No lecturing, criticizing, sarcasm, or questions! Do not say something like, "Will you please just eat your breakfast?" Instead, say "You've got 5 minutes to eat your breakfast" or "Put your pants on now." Keep your commands brief and do not keep repeating yourself. If your child listened to your command, then give praise. If your child did not listen to your command, then the disincentives you have already set up will automatically kick in.

When you give a command to your child, make sure you have his undivided attention. Do not give a command when your child is preoccupied with something like a cell phone. Instead, say to your child, "Look at me," get his full attention, and then give your command. If you are unsure whether your child fully listened or understood what you just said, then ask him to repeat what you just said. You can see why I want you to budget plenty of time for the morning routine!

Make sure as well that you are giving your child commands that he *can actually do*. Parents sometimes load their child with things to do and then get frustrated when everything is not done. A parent might say, "Go into your room, get dressed, brush your teeth, and comb your hair." Ten minutes later, when the boy is dressed but just sitting on his bed, his father might become upset! A better way to do this is to give your child *one step to do at a time*. You could say "Go into your room and get dressed now" and then check on your child 10 minutes later to give the next command ("Good job. Now go brush your teeth."). And so on. Remember that a 7- or 8-year-old does not think and remember the way you do, so keep it simple!

I also suggest that you do with your child whatever you want him to do. Brush your teeth together, get dressed at the same time in separate rooms, eat breakfast together, and pack up work materials/purses and backpacks together. If you keep the same general routine as your child, then you can better monitor how well he is doing. You will also serve as a good model for when that step should be done. And most kids, especially those who like attention, certainly enjoy doing things (even little things) with their parents.

During the morning routine and as your child goes to school, be sure to praise and give formal rewards for good behavior and disincentives for inappropriate behavior. In addition, maintain your voice in an *even and calm manner*. Try not to get upset or raise your voice. Instead, adopt a neutral, low-key, matter-of-fact tone. I like to think of it as the "You're going to school, end of story" tone. No arguing or begging, just the simple expectation that your child is going to school no matter what. End of story. Doing so will get across to your child your expectation that he should complete the morning routine and go to school. Do not yell or threaten your child; let the rewards and disincentives that you set up beforehand do your talking for you. Your child is dancing to *your* tune!

Repeated Statements/Questions and Calls/Texts

You may find, even after the morning routine is in place and your child is going to school, that he is still constantly pestering you with the same questions over and over or calling or texting you constantly from school. Children who refuse school for attention often do these kinds of things. They may continually whine in the morning and say things like, "I don't want to go to school. Can't I just stay home today? Mom, I want to stay home today. Please! I want to stay with you," and on and on and on—how draining.

Should I Skip Work to Go to School With My Child?

When young children refuse school for attention, parents often wonder whether they should miss work to go to school with their child. Many kids say they will go to school if only Mom or Dad goes with them and stays for most of the morning, for lunch, or even for most of the school day. Some parents "volunteer" as room helpers so they can justify being in their child's classroom and to make the morning routine so much easier.

I do not recommend that parents skip work or make extra efforts to be at school with their child. Doing so only reinforces the child's dependence or attention-seeking behavior and will make it that much harder later to get a child to attend school on his own. Be very clear with your child about what your boundaries are. You may tell your son that you are willing to walk him to the school's playground or main lobby and that is as far as you will go. You should arrange for a school official to then escort your child to class.

What if you *have* been spending class time with your child? If this is the case, then start to gradually withdraw yourself from your child's classroom or school. If you have been staying there for 2 hours (120 minutes), then try to leave after an hour and 45 minutes (105 minutes). As your child is able to handle this, continue to leave 15 minutes earlier every few days or so. If your child can handle your presence for 105 minutes after a few days, then cut your time to 90 minutes. Gradually work backward until you are able to drop off your child at the school playground or main lobby and have him or her escorted to class. If your child shows any disruptive behavior, then set up home-based disincentives for the behavior.

Constantly responding to these repeated statements and questions will wear you out, so don't do it. Respond *once* to your child's statement or question about school. You can say something like, "Yes, we've talked about this before. You are going to school today. End of story." *After that, ignore your child's repeated statements and questions.* If you continue to respond, then the attention you are giving will reinforce your child's behavior. Ignoring the behavior will help reduce these statements and questions over time.

What about persistent calls or texts to you from school? Many kids bring cell phones to school and make many calls or texts to their parents. If this is the case for you, then set a clear limit about how many times your child can call or text you and under what circumstances. I recommend that your child call or text you no more than twice per day (once in the morning and once in the afternoon) and *only* during times when the call or text is allowed at school and does not interfere with classroom activity. Check with school officials to see when a good and allowed time for a call or text would be.

Your child should be allowed to call or text you *only* if he is having a good day at school, so set up these calls or texts *only after* you have talked to your child's teacher or school counselor. If your child is calling or texting to get out of school or to ask you to pick him up early, then do not allow this. Simply tell your child that he must stay in school and that you will pick him up (or see him later) at the usual time. If necessary, end the communication yourself. If your child keeps calling or texting inappropriately, then be sure to provide a consequence for this behavior later that evening.

Running Away From the School Building

A particularly dangerous behavior involves a child's willingness to run out of the school building. Most children who refuse school for attention do spend the entire day in the classroom *once they get there*. Other kids, though, look to run out the door or slip away from the playground and go down the street. Some of these kids hide, but many try to find their way home. Of course, this behavior must be addressed as soon as it happens!

If you feel your child may run away from the school building, then you must meet with school officials immediately. *Keep in mind three main things*. First, be sure a plan is put in place that involves greater monitoring of your child during the school day. Once school officials know that a child is a "flight risk," they should take extra precautions to make sure the child does not leave the school building early again. Make sure you are comfortable with whatever plan is proposed but I recommend the plan *at least* include adult escorts from class to other areas of the school building, someone waiting for your child outside the restroom, and teachers or others keeping an "eagle eye" on your child during lunch, recess, and other nonclassroom times.

Second, develop a plan for what happens if your child does somehow leave the school campus. Each school district typically has its own policy and response system for this event. You should be notified immediately as well. If your child does somehow make it home and you are there, then bring him back to school and let school officials know where he is and what happened. Then investigate what went wrong and how it could be prevented in the future.

Third, let school officials know when your child is going to be absent on a given day. That way, they won't be looking for your child if he is not there. In addition, make it a habit of going to the front office to let someone in charge know that your child is now in school, even if he is late. The goal is to set up a system where you and school officials always know where your child is and, if he is not where he is supposed to be, then to make sure that everyone knows right away what has happened so he can be found.

Separation Anxiety and "Clingy" Behavior

Most of this chapter has been devoted to your child's attention-seeking behavior, which is a main problem in younger children with school attendance problems. As mentioned in Chapter 2, some of these kids also have separation anxiety or great worry about harm happening to parents or to the child when separation occurs. Many kids with separation anxiety worry about their parents being in a car accident and not being able to pick them up from school.

If your child has separation anxiety, then he may insist that you be at school by a certain time to pick him up. Many kids insist that a parent pick them up at a very specific time like 3:17 p.m. Many parents will respond to this by making sure they are there by 3:17 p.m. and even rearranging their afternoon schedule to accommodate this. If you are doing something like this, however, you are "dancing to your child's tune" instead of the other way around.

Children must learn to be flexible and understand that terrible things are not likely to happen if a parent is a few minutes late picking them up. If your child has this issue, then ask him to wait for you at a safe spot at school. Examples include the main office or lobby, school playground, or front door. Tell your child that you will not be more than 15 minutes late but that you will pick him up at different times. If your child is ready by 3:17 p.m., you will be there anytime between 3:17 p.m. and 3:32 p.m. Then, vary the times that you pick your child up. Come one day at 3:22, another day at 3:30, and another day at 3:17 p.m. (it's okay to be on time occasionally!). Ignore tantrums and complaints about this.

When you do pick up your child from school, remind him that nothing bad happened. As you practice this more, your child will become less tense and realize that bad things are not likely to happen. As he can tolerate these different times, praise him for being brave. Also, in case you are ever later than 3:32 p.m., give your child a strategy for what to do. Your child could speak to someone in the main office about the fact you are late (only past 3:32 p.m. in this example). That way, he will feel safe until you or someone else does come to pick him up. If your child has a cell phone, then you can call/text and tell him that you will be there a little past 3:32 p.m. (or whatever time applies to your situation).

Other kids with separation anxiety cling tightly to their parents in the morning. Some of this behavior is for attention, and some of it is due to distress. However, your response should be the same. If your child clings to you on the playground before school, then set up a regular routine for the drop off just as you did for the morning at home. For example,

- Ask your child *at home* if he has everything needed for school. Do not allow your child to later go back home to retrieve something; if something was forgotten, tell your child that he has to go to school on time but that you will bring the item to school later *if possible*. If you do this, then bring the item to the main office and not to your child directly.
- Say final goodbyes and give final affections *at home* and not at school.
- Arrive at the school playground at the same time each school day and preferably 10 minutes before your child is expected to enter the school building.
- Without much discussion, walk your child to the playground or wherever children have to line up to go into the school building. Do this about 5 minutes before your child is expected to enter the school building. Ignore whining, crying, minor physical complaints, and statements or questions about wanting to go home or not be in school.

- Even if your child is crying or clingy, praise him for being brave and going to school. Remember, you always want to get across your point that school attendance is expected.
- Arrange to have a friendly school official (preferably one known and liked by your child) come outside or stand in the school doorway to greet your child, smile, and escort him to class.
- Leave quickly.

Do not allow your child to come with you to the car and do not drive your child back home. If for some reason you absolutely cannot get your child into the school building on time, then stay there as long as necessary, even a couple of hours, to get your child to eventually go into the school building. It is far better for your child (and for you tomorrow) to enter school at 10:30 a.m. and stay the rest of the day than to miss the entire day of school and be home. Remember also to provide a disincentive later that evening for any delays going to school. I know this can be hard to do. In many cases, though, children are upset for a few minutes inside the school building and are then fine for the rest of the school day.

If you are worried, then you may contact your child's teacher or school counselor later that morning to see how your child is doing and to ease your concerns about his mood. If you discover that your child is still crying at lunchtime and beyond, then try some of the methods in Chapter 3. If your child goes to school and sobs continually or is highly distressed for the entire day, then you may wish seek the help of a qualified mental health professional (see Chapter 1). In general, though, the more you practice this entering-school routine and the more you tell your child that you expect him to go to school, the easier it will be for him to enter school.

Physically Bringing a Child to School

What if you cannot get your child out of the home to even try the entering-school routine? Parents often ask me in this situation,

"Should I just bring my child to school?" Physically bringing a child to go to school can be tricky, so I do not recommend it except under very specific circumstances. My preference is to set up the morning routine, apply the rewards and disincentives, and tell your child that you expect him to go to school. Allow these methods to take their course for at least a few weeks before moving on to what is described next.

If you have a particularly willful child who absolutely refuses to leave the home or car, then you might consider physically bringing him to school. However, I recommend doing so only as a last resort and under *all* of the following conditions:

- Your child is not older than age 10 years.
- Your child has no distress whatsoever about school (see Chapters 3 and 4).
- Your child is refusing school *only* for attention from you.
- Your child fully understands what will happen if he does not leave home or the car.
- Your child is missing more school days than he goes.
- Two adults can take your child to school *every day*.
- School officials have been notified of your plan and have agreed to meet you at your car or the entrance to the school building to escort your child to class.
- You have no guilt, distress, hesitation, or reservations about doing this.
- You have the energy and ability to do this.

If any of these do not apply to your situation, then I do not recommend physically bringing your child to school. If you try this approach, however, this is what I recommend at the end of the morning routine:

- Tell your child in advance that you will physically take him to school if he refuses to leave home or the car. If your child does start to refuse to do so, then give one warning: "Go now or we will take you there."

- If necessary, have two adults (possibly including yourself) take your child to the car and place him in the backseat with another adult who can sit with him and prevent him from leaving the car. Do not do this on your own!
- Drive your child to school and ignore crying, tantrums, and other disruptive behaviors. Stay calm, neutral, and matter of fact in your tone of voice. In this situation, it is usually best not to say anything at all.
- Bring your child to the school entrance, where a school official can meet him and escort him to class. Leave quickly and do not worry about saying goodbye or exchanging hugs if your child is having a temper tantrum.
- Contact school officials later that morning to see what happened once you left. Provide a disincentive later that evening for your child's morning disruptive behavior.

If you are unsure about using this method, then do not do it. Physically bringing a child to school can effective, but the danger is that parents will hesitate or give up on doing it. If this happens, then a child's school refusal behavior is greatly reinforced, and it will be much harder for him to go back to school later. If you have a particularly difficult situation and are not sure about this approach, then use the other methods described in this chapter, speak with school officials about your options (see next section), or consult with a qualified mental health professional (see Chapter 1).

Missing Most of the School Day

If your child is missing most or all of the school day, then the first step toward full-time school attendance should be small. See what time of day your child seems most willing to go to school and use that as a starting point. Then you can gradually increase the amount of time your child spends in school.

My Child Is Home From School: What Now?

If your child is home from school or at your work because it was not possible to get him in the school building, then have him work on academic
tasks and materials during the hours he would normally be at school. Try
to limit fun activities or access to electronic devices for amusement. In addition, keep verbal and physical attention toward your child to a minimum.
Children who refuse school for attention want your attention. If they do not
get much of your attention for missing school, then they will be less likely
to refuse school.

If your child is at home or your workplace during the day, then have him
complete schoolwork or do other academic tasks, such as reading books,
finishing math worksheets, and writing. If others are watching your child,
then ask them to follow these recommendations. Following the end of
normal school hours, say after 3 p.m., a disincentive for missing school
can be provided, such as completing a chore. When your child does go to
school, be sure to give praise and more formal rewards and remind your
child that this is the kind of behavior you like to see.

If your child is missing most or all of the school day, then pursuing
a part-time schedule at first is a good idea. As mentioned in
Chapter 3, the first step in a part-time schedule can involve one of
the following:

- Your child goes to school in the morning and is then allowed to
  come home within an hour (then you gradually work forward
  by adding more time).
- Your child goes to school at 2 p.m. and is then allowed to come
  home when school normally ends, say at 3:10 (then you gradually work backward by adding more time).
- Your child goes to school only for lunch and is then allowed
  to come home afterward (then you gradually add more school
  time before and after lunch).

- Your child goes to school only for his favorite class or time of day (then you gradually add more classes or school time).
- Your child attends a school room other than his classroom, such as the school library, school counselor or nurse's office, or main lobby (then gradually add more classroom time).

I covered these steps at length in Chapter 3 so I will not repeat myself here. If your child is missing most of the school day, then I invite you to read Chapter 3, and, in particular, the section on changing the "doing" part of distress. This section will give you detailed ideas about how to set up a part-time attendance schedule that will eventually lead to full-time attendance. Continue to practice all of the methods described in this chapter, including setting up the morning routine and giving rewards, disincentives, and good commands. Even if your child is not currently going to school, continue with the morning routine and practice other methods during the day.

Do's and Don'ts!

I know that I have given you a lot of information in this chapter. Here is a list of some do and don't reminders.

Do:

- Set up a regular morning routine that allows plenty of time for everyone to get ready for school and work.
- Reward your child for properly getting ready in the morning and completing the morning routine.
- Provide a disincentive for not completing the morning routine or for refusing to enter school.
- Give rewards and disincentives in the morning and evening.
- Praise good behavior and ignore inappropriate behavior.
- Expect your child to go to school each day.
- Work closely with school officials when developing your morning plan.

- Speak to your child in a calm, matter-of-fact tone and give brief commands.
- Limit calls/texts and statements and questions about going to school.
- Set up a plan to deal with running away from school.
- Seek support from others, especially for the morning routine.
- Pursue a part-time school attendance schedule if necessary.
- Be consistent and use these methods every day.

Don't:
- Argue, yell, lecture, criticize, negotiate, beg, or bribe your child to go to school.
- Dance to your child's tune.
- Stay with your child at school.
- Linger at school or the playground when your child is supposed to enter school.
- Allow your child to come home early.
- Visit your child at school during the day.
- Physically bring your child to school unless all of the conditions mentioned previously apply.

Other Skills

Attention-seeking elementary schoolchildren sometimes lose ability in certain skills if they have missed a lengthy time at school. These skills can include attending school all day without contacting one's parents, participating in extracurricular activities, going on school field trips or related activities, sleeping overnight at a friend's home, staying home alone if appropriate, handling difficult or unpredictable situations, solving problems independently, or speaking to classmates at school. If this is the case for your child, then work with school officials to improve these skills or seek consultation from a qualified mental health professional (see Chapter 1).

Final Comments

Dealing with children who refuse school for attention takes a lot of work and patience. You will find yourself truly tested during those mornings when you are trying to ignore inappropriate behavior, tune out the screaming, and put aside your own doubts and guilt. Be sure to get help from other people if you need it. The most important thing to remember is to *be consistent and persistent!* The more you try these methods *every day*, even if it takes a few weeks, the more likely you will see your child more easily go to school. Hang in there! You can do it!

6

The Disengaged Middle/High School Adolescent

Maya is a 16-year-old girl who has been skipping afternoon classes to hang out with her friends outside of school. Although Maya does go to school in the morning, she often meets up with her friends Callie and Nita in the middle of the day for lunch off campus. Many times the teens eat and then "ditch" the rest of the day to go to a local shopping center or spend time at Callie's home. Maya is not distressed about school but complains that school is boring. She tried to hide her absences from her parents, but the principal recently informed Maya's mother that her daughter has now missed 9 days of school.

This chapter will be *more helpful to* you if your child's situation matches Maya's situation or if one of the following is true:

- Your child is refusing school *only* to do fun things outside of school during school hours.
- Your child is skipping class to be with friends or to do other fun things.
- Your child prefers to sleep in during the morning instead of going to school.
- Your child is generally disengaged from school.

This chapter will be *less helpful* to you if one of the following is true:

- Your child is refusing school *only* because she is very distressed about something related to school (see Chapter 3).
- Your child is refusing school *only* because she is very distressed about social or performance situations at school (see Chapter 4).
- Your child is refusing school *only* for attention from you or a significant other (see Chapter 5).

In Chapter 2 we discussed different reasons why children and adolescents have trouble going to school. One reason is that some teenagers like Maya enjoy doing fun activities outside of school during school hours. Maya enjoyed hanging out with her friends and spending time at another's home. Other kids miss school because they enjoy sleeping late, accessing electronic devices, or engaging in dangerous activities.

Children who miss school to do fun things outside of school during school hours are often older and try to keep their absences secret. These kids may or may not show disruptive behavior but may argue with their parents and others so that their absences can continue. Maya greatly enjoyed her time with friends and did not want that time to end. However, she and her mother had intense arguments about the value of an education and about going to school. Maya's mother insisted that her daughter go to school, but Maya found school to be "stupid" and did not see the point of graduating. Instead, she was greatly tempted by her friend's offers to leave school.

Many of these adolescents are *not particularly distressed about* school. If you feel that your child *is* distressed about school, then read Chapters 3 and 4. In addition, many of these adolescents do not seek attention from their parents or other adults. If you feel your child does seek your attention when missing school, then read Chapter 5.

To change your child's outlook about going to school and to help improve her school attendance, I concentrate on the following:

- Monitoring your child
- Setting up regular meetings with your child

- Developing written agreements for getting ready for school and for going to school
- Escorting your child from class to class
- Knowing what your child can say to friends who want him to leave school
- Changing what you say to your child
- Helping your child be more engaged at school

Why Am I Doing This?

If your child resembles Maya, then she may be quite good at slipping away from school and spending time with friends or doing other activities. You may be particularly frustrated and confused about this secretive behavior and may be angry at school officials for not watching your child more closely or for not letting you know what's been going on. All of this is understandable.

We have to change some things in this situation. First, we must make sure that you or school officials (or both) know *exactly where your child is at all times of the day*. This will require a lot of cooperation between you and school officials, so please focus on maintaining a good relationship with those at school. We need to develop a regular system of communication and watchfulness to minimize school attendance problems.

Another thing we have to change is moving the reward system away from missing school and toward attending school. Right now your child gets a lot of rewards for being out of school and perhaps little reward for being in school. This is kind of normal: Many of us take our child's school attendance for granted and pay less attention to it until absences become a problem. Your child is having trouble staying in school, so this needs to change. We have to set up a situation where your child is getting more reward for going to school and better enjoys going to school.

Another issue unique to this group is that teenagers like Maya often have peers that tempt them to ditch school. Maya usually left school after her friends encouraged her to skip classes. We may need to change what your child says and does to decline offers to miss school and attend class instead.

Finally, you and your child may be arguing a lot about school attendance. Again, this is understandable given how frustrating this situation can be. I make some suggestions as well about how you and your child can reach a reasonable agreement about school attendance and your teenager's activities outside of school.

All of these recommendations will require a lot of effort on your part. The methods in this chapter will be helpful *only* if you and/or your spouse/partner:

- Have the *will and the ability* to carry out the methods
- Support each other
- Are confident that your teen is refusing school *only* to do fun things outside of school during school hours or is disengaged from school
- Are working closely with school officials
- Can commit to doing the methods consistently and permanently
- Have a fairly good relationship with your child

Monitoring Your Child

Parents are often shocked to learn that their child has been skipping school. Once you have discovered this problem, you must work hard to know where your child is *at all times of the day* and not just during school hours. If your child is starting to leave the school campus, then we want to make sure we catch this as quickly as possible so she does not miss a large part of the school day.

How can we do this? The following are some suggestions:

- Meet with your teenager's teachers, school counselor, and other relevant school officials to make sure you are informed *immediately* when she has skipped school. Some schools are able to "keep an eye" on a particular child, and others are not. At a minimum, you want to know *as soon as possible* if your child has missed a class.

- If school officials say they can "keep an eye" on your child, then set up a system whereby someone is watching your child during times *when she is most likely* to leave the school campus. Often this occurs after lunch, but your child may leave school at certain times in the morning or afternoon as well. If your child is seen leaving the school campus, then she can be brought back into school (and face possible consequences). If you do not know when your child usually leaves school, or if your child leaves school at different times of the day, then make sure she is monitored as much as possible throughout the day.

- Ask your child to call/text you or contact a school official during a time at school when she is often absent. Many kids such as Maya are absent in the afternoon, so you may require your child to visit the school counselor's office at 1 and 2 to make sure she is actually in school. If she does not show up at these times, then you should be told right away. If your child leaves at different times of the school day, then she can check in with you or a school official once per hour.

- Require that your child keep an "attendance log" that is signed by each teacher. Your child should get each teacher's signature to show that she was in class and then show you this log each night. Work with school officials to set this up. A sample attendance log is provided (Worksheet 6.1). Feel free to photocopy this worksheet as much as you need or download multiple copies from the companion website (www.oxfordclinicalpsych.com/schoolattendance). A good rule of thumb is that a lack of signature for whatever reason is the same as a missed class. Do not accept excuses for a missed signature.

- As much as possible, find out where your child is likely to go when out of school. Many kids pick the same spot, but others roam around. Get names, addresses, and contact and other information about where your child is likely to be if not in school. This will help you find your child more quickly if necessary. *If you know your child has left the school campus, then try to bring her back to school if possible during school hours.*

Worksheet 6.1
Daily Attendance Log

Class (Starting With First Period)	Teacher's Name	Teacher's Signature and Date
_____	_____	_____
_____	_____	_____
_____	_____	_____
_____	_____	_____
_____	_____	_____
_____	_____	_____
_____	_____	_____
_____	_____	_____

- Be in the practice of knowing where your child is *even during nonschool hours*. Require your child to check in with you when out with friends and get names, addresses, and contact information regarding places where your child plans to be. If your child does not check in with you at set times, say every hour or so, then find her and bring her home. Set a curfew that is early on school nights and perhaps a bit later on Friday and Saturday nights.

The most important thing to remember is that you should know at all times where your child is and, if you do not know, to find her and to bring her to school or home. I know this requires a lot of effort on your part. Talk to others who can help locate your child and bring her to school or home. Enlist the help of school officials, grandparents and other relatives, friends, and neighbors. Stay in close contact with the parents of your child's friends. Get to know them well and set up a system where you are contacted immediately if your child goes somewhere she is not supposed to be. *If your child expects to be closely watched, especially at school, then she will be less likely to leave school.*

Regular Meetings

Further in this chapter I ask you to negotiate solutions to your child's problems getting ready for school and going to school. To do this, you must have regular meetings with your child to discuss school preparation and attendance and what can be done to improve these behaviors. I recommend that you meet with your child once per evening for at least a few minutes. Ask for the attendance log if you have asked her to complete one. Talk about what happened at school that day, what homework she has, what problems came up that day, and whether she was tempted to miss school.

You must have regular meetings with your child to discuss school preparation and attendance.

Try to make these meetings as stress-free as possible. Keep in mind that your goal is to support your child and her attempts to go to school. You may have discovered at this point that lecturing, criticizing, demanding, yelling, and punishing do not work. Instead, you will have to negotiate solutions to different problems *with your teenager*. Let your child know the following: "I'm willing to work with you to spend time with friends *as long as* you work with me to go to school." In addition, let your child know that you will help her handle problems related to school attendance such as makeup work that may be due. All of these problems are fixable if you and your child work together and if you seek the help of school officials.

Agreements for School Preparation and Attendance

When children become teenagers, parents find it harder to simply tell their kids what to do. Teenagers are growing up quickly and often want to be adults as fast as possible! This means reaching for independence in different ways. This is normal, and many parents allow their teenagers more freedom to spend time with friends, begin dating, or start driving a car. On the other hand, some teenagers end up doing things like skipping school. We have to find a good balance of what your teenager wants to do and what she is allowed to do.

Another thing that parents do differently with teenagers than younger kids is to *negotiate solutions to problems.* You might be able to order a 7-year-old to clean her room, but doing so with a 17-year-old can lead to a lot of arguing and stress. What many parents find is that they have to *work out some agreement with* their teenagers. A parent and teenager might agree that, in exchange for keeping her room clean, the teenager can go out with her friends on Friday night under certain conditions, such as being home by 11 p.m., texting home every hour, and letting parents know of any change in plans.

A teenager who is skipping school should be approached in the same way. We must recognize that your teenager wants independence, and we must recognize that the best way to reduce school absences is to negotiate a solution to the problem. You will not need to cave in to outrageous demands from your child, but you will want to reach an agreement that gives her what she wants, such as some independence, under certain conditions that you want, such as getting ready for school in the morning and staying in school for the entire day.

How can we do this? I recommend that you and your child develop *written agreements*. A written agreement is one that that you and your child work out together to make sure everyone gets what they want. Developing these agreements will take a lot of effort on your part and your child's part, and I recommend that they be part of the evening discussion you have with your child (see previous section).

What does a written agreement look like? A sample is provided here. The agreement should be simple and include four basic things. *First*, a "privileges" column contains *the kinds of things your child wants*. These privileges can be things that your child can touch and see, such as time with friends, access to electronic devices, money, or other special items. Allow only those privileges that fit within your family's value system and budget.

Second, a "responsibilities" column will contain *the kinds of things that you want*. The things you want should also be things that can be touched and seen, such as getting out of bed on time, getting ready for school on time, staying in school for an entire day, and completing a certain chore at home. Choose just a few responsibilities to start; we need to take things one step at a time.

Third, the agreement has a place where you and your child can sign and date the agreement. This helps make the agreement "official" and makes it something you can rely on instead of arguing. Let the agreement and the fact that everyone signed it do your talking for you. If your child complains about going to school, then point to the agreement! *Fourth*, the agreement will have a general statement where privileges and responsibilities are made a little clearer (see further section on Step 1 of the agreement).

Sample Agreement

Privileges   *Responsibilities*

General Statements

Everyone who signs this agreement agrees to the conditions of this agreement and to read and initial the agreement every day.

Child's signature: _____

Parent's signature: _____

Date: _____

Working Together on an Agreement

A written agreement is one that you and your child develop to ease tension and give everyone most of what they want. An agreement is *not* a document that contains only what *one party* wants. If your child will not work with you on the agreement, or has unreasonable demands, then something other than the agreement will need to be tried (see methods described in this and other chapters). On the other hand, if you make too many demands of your child, then the agreement process also will not work. Give and take on your part and your child's part is needed for agreements to be successful.

During your discussions with your child, ask her to write a list of things that she wants. Note that I did not say a list of things she wants in return for going to school. Instead, she should give you a list of things that she would enjoy doing *in general* and that you can use as part of the agreement. Likewise, you should write a list of things that you want. Keep your list simple and *stick to three main topics*: a basic chore such as taking out the garbage, getting ready for school on time in the morning, and staying in school for an entire day. If you and your child become good at using agreements once school attendance improves, then you can focus on other areas of disagreement.

Once you have these lists, you and your child can review each one. Take any item off the list that is unreasonable, such as going to school only 2 out of every 5 days. Make it clear to your child that she is expected to get ready for school and stay in school the entire day, and that you are willing to make sure that she will get some of what she wants if she does this. Once you have your final lists set, you are ready to try your first agreement. Let's go to Step 1.

Step 1: A Simple Agreement

Your first agreement with your teenager should be a *simple one* that is likely to succeed. You and your child may agree on one chore. Your child could agree to take out the garbage on Tuesday and Friday, and you could agree that, if she does, she can go out with friends under certain conditions on Friday night. You and your child must also agree about what will happen if the garbage is *not taken out* on Tuesday or Friday. In this case, you and your child could agree that she would need to stay in Friday night. *Do not start with a complicated agreement!*

If you and your child reach an agreement like this, then the privileges and responsibilities could be formally written (see Figure 6.1). As you write out the agreement, be sure that you and your child *go over every word* to make sure there are no misunderstandings. Ask your child if she has questions or changes and make changes if necessary.

Be sure that you and your child are completely comfortable with every word of the agreement. You do not want your child to quickly agree just so she can leave the meeting and you will not want to complete the agreement if you cannot follow through with its conditions. Instead, make sure that you and your child fully agree with the wording of the agreement and *encourage your child to sign the agreement only when she feels the agreement is completely fair.* Once

Privileges	Responsibilities
For the privilege of going out with her friends on Friday night,	*Maya agrees to take out the garbage on Tuesday before 7 p.m. and on Friday before 7 p.m.*
General statements	

Should Maya not complete this duty on Tuesday or Friday, then she will be grounded Friday night.

Mom will check at 7 p.m. on Tuesday and Friday to make sure the garbage was taken out.

Maya must be home on Friday night by 11, be with Callie and Nita only at the movie theatre, and call home every hour to check in.

This contract is good only for this week.

Everyone who signs this contract agrees to the conditions of this contract and to read and initial the contract every day.

Child's signature: _____

Parent's/parents' signature(s): _____

Date: _____

Figure 6.1 Sample first agreement (chore).

Privileges	Responsibilities
For the privilege of staying up, until 10 p.m on a particular night,	*Maya agrees to rise from bed no later than 6.50 a.m. that morning.*
General statements	
If Maya does not rise from bed by 6.50 a.m., she must go to bed that evening at 8.30 p.m.	
Rising from bed means that Maya's entire body is out of bed by 6.50 a.m.	
Mom will make sure Maya's alarm is set and that she wakes Maya by 6.40 a.m.	
This contract is good only for this week (Monday-Friday).	
Everyone who signs this contract agrees to the conditions of this contract and to read and initial the contract every day.	
Child's signature: _____	
Parent's/parents' signature(s): _____	
Date: _____	

Figure 6.2 Sample second agreement (school preparation: getting out of bed only).

everyone feels the agreement is completely fair, then they can sign the agreement.

Be sure that each agreement you develop, including this one, has a short timeline of no more than 1 week. The sample agreement in Figure 6.2 could be tried for 5 days (Monday to Friday of a certain week) and expire after Friday. This allows you and your child to see what went right and what went wrong and to make changes to the agreement as needed.

Now you are ready to put the agreement into action and see what happens. One of three things is likely to happen:

- The agreement worked well: The garbage was taken out, and your child had a fun night with her friends on Friday night! The best possible scenario!
- Someone did not fulfill one end of the agreement: The garbage was not taken out or the garbage was taken out but your child was not allowed to go out on Friday night.
- The agreement was forgotten or did not work for some reason.

Let's talk about each of these separately. If the agreement worked, great! Be sure to praise your child (and yourself) for agreeing to do something and following through on the agreement. If this happened, then sit down with your child and say how glad you are that you and she were able to negotiate a solution to a problem. This is much better than arguing, so good job! I recommend two things at this point. First, extend this first agreement to another Monday-to-Friday period or whatever week you choose. Second, go to Step 2 (see further section).

If someone did not fulfill one end of the agreement, find out why. Why was the garbage not taken out? Did your child forget? Was the task too hard? Did she simply not care about the agreement or about going out Friday night? Do not have this discussion until the agreement is officially over. Do not nag your child to take out the garbage on the day she is supposed to do so—*let the agreement and its conditions do your talking for you!* Watch your own behavior as well; be sure to follow through on any rewards that are due your child. If you promised a Friday night with friends, and she earned it, then give her a Friday night with friends.

In this situation, rework the agreement so your child is able to receive its rewards. You may have to make the agreement or the task simpler and easier to remember. Or you may have to "tweak" or increase the rewards and consequences to make them more effective. Some children fail the first agreement because they are testing their parents: Will Mom let me go out anyway even if I didn't take out the garbage? If this is the case, then stick to the agreement. If your child did not do what she agreed to do, then go ahead with the consequences (loss of time with friends in this case). If your child is willing to try the agreement or some simpler agreement again, then do so. If your child is unwilling to try another agreement, then you may wish to use the other methods described in this and other chapters.

Finally, the agreement may have been forgotten or did not work for some reason. We lead busy lives, so the agreement may have gotten pushed to the side. I recommend in this case that you and your child read and initial the agreement *every day* to remind yourselves of its privileges and responsibilities. Post the agreement on the refrigerator so that it is plain to see. Find out why the agreement did not work and write a new one that has a better chance of working. *Agreements will work only if they are taken seriously.*

Once you have some success with this first, simple agreement, go to Step 2. If you are having trouble with the first agreement, then continue writing agreements that involve small tasks like chores. You want to be sure that this first agreement goes well before tackling more difficult problems such as school preparation and attendance. In the meantime, work closely with school officials regarding the other methods in this chapter to avoid delays in having your child attend school full time.

Step 2: Getting Ready for School

If your first agreement went well and you and your child have agreed to continue with this method, then the next step involves getting ready for school. If your child has no problems getting ready for school, then you can go to Step 3 (see next section). If your child has trouble getting out of bed or has other problems getting ready in the morning, then this next agreement step is for you. If there is great urgency about increasing your child's school attendance at this point, then Steps 2 and 3 (see next section) may be combined.

Problems Getting Out of Bed

Some teenagers miss school because they have a lot of trouble getting out of bed in the morning. Teenagers do need a lot of sleep because their bodies are changing, but they still have to get up in the morning and go to school! If your child has this problem, then be sure she is getting plenty of sleep. The following will help:

- Make sure your child only *sleeps* in her bed and does not use it for other activities, such as accessing electronic devices or completing homework.

- Be sure your child is in bed *with lights out* at an appropriate time, say 8 to 9 hours before having to get up in the morning.
- Avoid caffeine, nicotine, alcohol, and exercise before bedtime.
- Practice relaxation methods close to bedtime (see Chapter 3).
- Follow the same routine before bedtime and begin this routine 30 minutes before lights out.
- Set curfew for at least 2 hours before bedtime.
- Speak to your pediatrician about sleep medication if necessary.

What if your child has trouble getting out of bed? Avoid drastic actions. Instead, get up early and wake your child in stages like a snooze alarm. If your child has to be up by 6 a.m., get up at 5:15 a.m. and wake your child at 5:30, 5:40, 5:50, 5:55, and 5:59 a.m. Tell your child how many minutes she has left before having to get up. Set a loud alarm as well across the room. If your child still won't get up, then continue to speak to her every 5 minutes. Set up agreements to give rewards and consequences for getting up or not getting up from bed. Finally, *do not give up and let your child sleep late and miss school completely.* Your child may finally get up and go to school an hour late, but this is better than missing the entire school day.

An agreement at this second step involves the same ideas as Step 1: meeting with your teenager, being specific about what you and she want, keeping the timeline of the agreement short, and developing a final agreement. An agreement at this point might be simple. You may agree with your daughter that she has to be out of bed by a certain time in the morning. If she does, then some good thing happens; if she does not, then some less-than-good thing happens (see Figure 6.2).

If your child has a lot of trouble getting ready for school in the morning, and not just getting out of bed, then you can build a morning routine into the agreement. The morning routine could be very similar to what I discussed in Chapter 5. Here is an example:

6:50 a.m.	Rise from bed
6:50–7 a.m.	Go to the bathroom and wash (10 minutes)
7–7:20 a.m.	Eat breakfast (which should be ready by 7 or whenever breakfast time starts) (20 minutes)
7:20–7:30 a.m.	Brush teeth in bathroom and wash as needed (10 minutes)
7:30–7:50 a.m.	Dress and accessorize for school (20 minutes)
7:50–8 a.m.	Make final preparations for school, such as putting on a jacket or getting backpack ready (10 minutes)
8–8:20 a.m.	Extra time (if child is ready, she can do what she wants inside the home; if child is not ready, she can use this time to finish) (20 minutes)
8:20–8:50 a.m.	Commute to school and child enters school (30 minutes)

Negotiate this morning routine with your teenager (this is different with younger kids and what I said in Chapter 5, where I encourage parents to simply tell their younger child what will happen in the morning). When you develop the agreement, keep it simple. You do not need to set up privileges and responsibilities for each step of the morning routine. Instead, use this routine as a guide or "road map" to set up privileges and responsibilities for being ready for school on time (Figure 6.3).

Once you have developed this agreement, put the agreement into action and see what happens. As mentioned before, let the agreement run its course and do not nag your child to get ready in the morning. Simply give the consequences listed in the agreement if she does not complete the morning routine. This may take some patience and persistence on your part and your child's part.

Privileges	Responsibilities
For the privilege of staying up until 10 p.m. on a particular night,	*Maya agrees to rise from bed no later than 6.50 a.m. that morning.*
For the privilege of having access to television and the computer that evening,	*Maya agrees to complete the morning routine by 8.20 a.m.*
For the privilege of having access to television, the computer, and telephone that evening,	*Maya agrees to complete the morning routine by 8 a.m.*

General statements

If Maya does not rise from bed by 6.50 a.m., she must go to bed that evening at 8.30 p.m.

Rising from bed means that Maya's entire body is out of bed by 6.50 a.m.

Mom will make sure Maya's alarm is set and that she wakes Maya by 6.40 a.m.

Mom will decide what time Maya is ready in the morning.

Mom and Maya can discuss whether Maya is done (and what else needs to be done) at 7.50 a.m. and 8.10 a.m. to give Maya a good chance being done by 8 or 8.20.

If Maya is not ready by 8 a.m., she loses access to television and the computer that evening.

If Maya is not ready by 8.20 a.m., she loses access to television, the computer, and telephone that evening.

This contract is good only for this week (Monday –Friday).

Everyone who signs this contract agrees to the conditions of this contract and to read and initial the contract every day.

Child's signature: _____

Parent's/parents' signature(s): _____

Date: _____

Figure 6.3 Sample second agreement (school preparation: completing the morning routine).

If the agreement is not working after a couple of weeks and your child is still unable to rise from bed or get ready on time, then rework the agreement so that it is simpler and easier for your child to do. You may have to "tweak" or increase the rewards and consequences to make them more effective. Be firm in your expectation that your child should be getting ready for school but recognize as well that changes might have to be made so she is able to receive the rewards in the agreement.

If your child can finally be ready by 10 a.m. and then go to school, then start at this point for the agreement and give rewards for being in school by 10 a.m. As she is able to be in school by 10, she can later be expected to be ready for school at gradually earlier times, such as 9:45, 9:15, and 8:45 a.m. These earlier times can be part of new agreements. A teenager who is getting ready for school and going to school for at least some of the day is preferable to one who cannot get ready at an early time, loses all agreement rewards as a result, and then will not go to school at all. *Be flexible in your thinking when writing agreements.* Once your child is able to rise from bed and get ready for school, then you may be ready for the third step, which involves improved school attendance.

Step 3: School Attendance

Agreements to improve your child's school attendance include the recommendations I made for Steps 1 and 2: negotiate the agreement with your child, rework the agreement (and its rewards and consequences) as necessary, keep the agreement simple, use a short timeline, and let the agreement do your talking for you. If your child is skipping only part of a school day or a class or two, then your first school attendance agreement could require your child to stay in school the entire day (Figure 6.4).

If your child is missing most or all of the school day, then the first school attendance agreement should involve some *small step* toward full-time school attendance. You can start with a part-time schedule and go from there. Ask your child what time of day is easiest for her to go to school. Teenagers such as Maya sometimes say they would go to school if school were held only in the morning. So I tell them: go to school for the morning! Find out what time of day your child is most willing to attend school and use that as a starting point. Then, using the agreements, gradually increase the amount of time your child spends in school.

Privileges	Responsibilities
For the privilege of seeing her friends on the weekend,	*Maya agrees to have no more than zero marked absences this week.*
For the privilege of being paid $10 for vacuuming the house on Saturday,	*Maya agrees to have no more than one marked class absence this week*
For the privilege of being paid $5 for vacuuming the house on Saturday,	*Maya agrees to have no more than two marked class absences this week.*

General statements

A marked absence is equal to one missed class and is determined by the school.

"Vacuuming the house" means vacuuming the family room, living room, all bedrooms, and the stairs and landing. Mom will check to see that the vacuuming was done well.

If Maya has one or more marked absences this week, she may not see her friends this weekend.

If Maya has two or more marked absences this week, she must vacuum the house for free. If she does not vacuum the house, then she loses her computer, television, and telephone.

This contract is good only for this week (Monday–Friday).

Everyone who signs this contract agrees to the conditions of this contract and to read and initial the contract every day.

Child's signature: _____

Parent's/parents' signature(s): _____

Date: _____

Figure 6.4 Sample third agreement (school attendance). *Note*: This agreement may be done in addition to the other agreements mentioned so far.

If your child is missing most or all of the school day, then pursuing a part-time schedule at first is a good idea. As mentioned in Chapter 3, the first step in a part-time schedule can involve one of the following:

- Having your child go to school in the morning and be allowed to come home within an hour (then gradually working forward by adding more time)

- Having your child go to school at 2 p.m. and be allowed to come home when school normally ends, say at 3:10 (then gradually working backward by adding more time)
- Having your child go to school only for lunch and be allowed to come home afterward (then gradually adding more school time before and after lunch)
- Having your child go to school only for her favorite class or time of day (then gradually adding more classes or school time)
- Having your child attend a school room other than her classroom, such as the school library, school counselor or nurse's office, or main lobby (then gradually adding more classroom time)

I covered these steps at length in Chapter 3, so I will not repeat myself here. If your child is missing most of the school day, then read Chapter 3 and, in particular, the section on changing the doing part of distress. This section will give you detailed ideas about how to set up a part-time attendance schedule that will eventually lead to full-time attendance.

As you are doing this, practice all of the methods described in this chapter, including setting up agreements and escorting a child from class to class (see next section). If your child is not currently going to school, then continue with the morning routine and practice other methods during the day (see Chapter 5).

Accommodation Plans

You may be facing a situation where your child has been out of school for some time, missing work has piled high, and your child is at risk of failing the rest of the school year. Many kids ask, "What is the point of going back to school if I can't get all the missing work done or if I'm going to fail the school year anyway?" This is a legitimate question.

In this situation, speak to school officials about the possibility of an accommodation plan that could include a "504 plan" or an "individualized education plan" (IEP). A 504 plan comes from a federal law that mandates school districts to accommodate students with some condition that interferes with learning. Examples include chronic medical conditions, depression or anxiety, or learning or attention deficit hyperactivity disorder. If your child might have one or more of these problems, then seek an evaluation from qualified medical and mental health professionals (see Chapter 1).

Accommodation plans may be used to change class schedules, makeup work, credits, or other conditions that might make it easier for your child to attend school. If your child can go to school at least part-time and complete some schoolwork, then this could be built into the accommodation plan. Be sure to work closely with school officials to see what your options are.

Escorting a Child From Class to Class

Your teenager may be willing to complete a school attendance agreement but is still tempted to miss school and does miss school. We do want your child to receive the agreement rewards for going to school. One suggestion to do so involves someone escorting your child from class to class. I discuss this recommendation in this section. A second recommendation involves teaching your child how to turn down offers to miss school. I discuss this recommendation in the next section.

Escorting a child from class to class is similar to the increased monitoring I discussed previously. We must make sure that we know where your child is at all times. But we also want your child to get the rewards for going to school. Even if your child is escorted from class to class, I count this as being in school. Therefore, your child is entitled to the rewards from the agreement.

What exactly does "escorting from class to class" mean? Escorting can involve the following:

- Going to school with your child and walking her from one class to another. If you are willing and able do this *and* school officials agree to let you do this, then great. But I understand that many parents do not see this as a good option because they have to go to work and do other things.

- Asking someone you know to walk your child from class to class. Some relatives, friends, or others have time during the day and could escort your child. Obviously this takes a lot of effort on the part of one person, so if different people could rotate doing the job, that would be great. But I understand that this option can be difficult to set up and maintain as well.

- Arranging with school officials to have someone at school escort your child from class to class. A classmate, peer, or other child *whom you trust to do the right thing* could do the escorting and report to you or to a school official any problems. On days your child misses school, this person could call your child that evening to encourage her to come to school the next day. Or a school official such as a counselor or some other adult could do the escorting. The last is sometimes tough to do because of the drain on the school official's time.

- Arranging with school officials to have each teacher of each class walk your child to her next class. In this situation, your child's first-period teacher walks your child (at the end of first period) to her second-period class. The second-period teacher then walks your child (at the end of second period) to her third-period class, and so on for the rest of the day. This type of escorting has the advantage of not laying the burden on one person. In addition, your child could more easily get each teacher to sign her attendance log. A problem is that teachers or others may be overly busy and are not always able to complete the escorting. See what can be arranged at your child's school.

A downside of escorting is that you or other people cannot escort your child forever. As your child receives rewards for being in school, the need for an escort should be less. If your child has been going to school for at least a couple of weeks with an escort, then you might be able to scale this back. Your child could be escorted in the morning but not the afternoon. Or she may be escorted only at "high-risk" times of the day, such as around lunchtime. If your child stays in school with a limited escort, then the escorting could end altogether. Remind your child that escorting can resume in the future as needed.

Declining Offers to Miss School

Your teenager may also need help knowing what to do or say to decline offers from others to miss school. Maya needed to know what she could do and say to Callie and Nita to decline their offers to miss school. She also needed to do this in a way that did not threaten her friendship with them but at the same time allowed her to stay in school.

I encourage teenagers to avoid situations at school that involve temptations to miss school. Find out what these high-risk situations are for your child. Sometimes lunch (or right after lunch) is the time students are most likely to see friends who want them to miss school. If this is the case, then see if your child can eat lunch elsewhere or at another time of day. Consult with school officials to see what changes can be made. Other kids say that they are approached at their locker and then feel compelled to leave school. In this situation, see if you and your child can rearrange her locker visits to help avoid this.

If your child is met with offers to miss school, then give her suggestions for what she can say in this situation to turn down these offers. *Keep in mind that your child does not want to look foolish in these situations.* The statements should thus be brief and clear and positive. Examples include the following: "I said I would stay in school to hang out this weekend"; "I can't, I've got that huge science project due Friday"; or "I have to get to class."

Talk to your child *each day* about any offers she had to miss school and how she responded. Do not criticize or lecture or take over the conversation. Instead, be supportive and help her develop ideas for doing or saying things differently to lower temptations to miss school. If she did turn down an offer to miss school, give lots of praise! Also, work closely with school officials to see what could be done to minimize your child's time with others who tempt her to miss school.

Changing What You Say to Your Child

If you and your child are arguing a lot, then I encourage you to use the methods in this chapter to negotiate solutions to different problems. Be patient and supportive while also firm and focused. Do not yell, nag, lecture, or criticize. Avoid interrupting, name-calling, accusations, threats, insults, sarcasm, silence, and dwelling on past failures or problems. None of these actions are productive. *Instead, focus on the immediate future and what can be done right now!* Encourage your child to participate in the agreement process, *listen carefully to what she has to say,* and praise her (and yourself) for good-faith attempts to solve difficult problems. You can do it!

On the other hand, you may find that your conflict with your teenager is so intense that it prevents you from using the agreements and other methods in this chapter. Some family members have a long history of arguing or have become so frustrated or pessimistic that it is too difficult to try different ways of communicating on their own. If this is the case for your family, then I recommend seeking the help of a qualified mental health professional (see Chapter 1).

Engagement Strategies

Some teenagers become bored and disengaged from school as they enter middle and high school. Grades may suffer, connections with peers and teachers may fade, and interest and motivation regarding school declines. If boredom and disengagement are issues for your teenager, then work with school officials on possible solutions:

- Arrange to have your teenager meet regularly with someone at school who can help with academic work, social problems, and even family challenges.
- Arrange tutoring so that your teenager is up to date on his schoolwork and feels comfortable knowing what is happening and being discussed in his classes.

- Discuss how your teenager's schoolwork is personally relevant, meaningful, and valuable, including showing him how different aspects of schoolwork apply to the real world.
- Reframe the purpose of school from a short-term sense of obligation and toward long-term opportunities for positive learning, self-fulfillment, problem-solving, skills building, and goal achievement.
- Work with schoolteachers and other officials to help provide more personalized attention and feedback to your teenager.
- Work with school officials to establish school-based incentives for attendance, choose elective classes of greater interest to your teenager, and increase involvement in extracurricular activities.

Do's and Don'ts!

I know that I have given you a lot of information in this chapter. The following is a list of some do and don't reminders:

Do:

- Monitor your child during the day and evening—always know where she is!
- Set up a system at school that helps prevent your child from leaving school.
- Have your child keep a regular attendance log.
- Set up regular evening meetings with your child to discuss agreements, what happened at school that day, homework, problems, and offers to miss school.
- Develop agreements for chores, school preparation, and school attendance.
- Find what rewards for going to school work best.
- Escort your child from class to class if necessary and possible so she can receive agreement rewards.
- Work with your child and with school officials so your child can more easily avoid or decline offers to miss school.
- Expect your child to go to school each day.

- Work closely with school officials when developing your plans.
- Speak to your child in a calm, matter-of-fact tone.
- Solve problems getting out of bed.
- Consider accommodation plans where appropriate.
- Be consistent and use the methods in this chapter every day.

Don't:
- Argue, yell, lecture, criticize, or physically punish your child to get her to go to school.
- Ignore your child's attendance problem during the day.
- Allow your child to do fun things outside of school during school hours.
- Forget any agreement you have written.
- Forget to give rewards that are due your child.

Other Skills

Disengaged middle/high school teenagers sometimes lose ability in certain skills if they have missed a lengthy time at school. These skills can include developing long-term plans after high school, managing changes in family relationships, dealing with multiple social challenges and mood changes, managing conflict with others, speaking with unknown authority figures, managing negative feedback or comments from others, handling difficult or unpredictable situations, or solving problems independently. If this is the case for your teenager, then work with school officials to improve these skills or seek consultation from a qualified mental health professional (see Chapter 1).

Final Comments

Dealing with children who are older and who skip school to do fun things outside of school during school hours can be tough. Solving this problem may take some time and will require a lot of effort on your part. As with any child with school attendance problems, be sure to rely a lot on the help of others and work closely with school officials and other professionals if necessary. Keep in mind as well that some of the topics covered in Chapter 8 may be especially relevant to the adolescents discussed in this chapter.

7

Prevention and Special Circumstances

In previous chapters I covered ways to manage your child's school attendance problems. In this chapter, I discuss:

- Preventing school attendance problems in the future
- Special circumstances regarding your family or your child
- What to do if you have not found the methods in this book to be very helpful

Preventing School Attendance Problems in the Future

If you helped your child return to school with less distress, congratulations! I am sure this required a lot of effort on your part, and you might be wondering, How do I keep it this way? Many parents are concerned about how to keep their child in school once he has gone back to school. This is a good concern. To help prevent school attendance problems in the future, please keep the following suggestions in mind.

You must continue to practice whatever methods helped get your child back to school. Some families assume, once the attendance crisis is over, that things can go "back to normal." Other parents want to "leave well enough alone" and not discuss possible attendance problems or they ignore warning signs of new school attendance problems. The problem with going back to normal and being less vigilant is that this increases the chance of having more problems in the future and going back to arguing, bribery, tension, and old ways of dealing with absenteeism.

Instead, you must practice *every day* those methods that were successful in getting your child back to school. I know this is a lot of work, but the alternative, which means going through this all over again, is worse and will cause you tremendous distress. In addition, you must constantly pay attention to warning signs that might indicate another attendance problem. Examples include increased stress, physical complaints, statements about not wanting to go to school, and difficulty getting ready in the morning.

If your child was generally distressed about school, then he should continue to practice methods to ease physical "feelings" of distress and continue to attend school to manage these uncomfortable feelings. If your child was distressed about social and performance situations at school, then he should continue to practice these methods of relaxation in addition to ways of thinking more realistically (the "STOP" method). If your child refused school for your attention, then you should continue to use the structured morning routine, rewards, disincentives, and brief commands. If your child missed school to do fun things outside of school during school hours, then you should continue to monitor his whereabouts and attendance, develop agreements, escort him to school and class when necessary, help him decline offers to miss school, and boost his engagement at school.

I strongly recommend that you periodically reread relevant sections of this book. Pick which chapter or which section of the book seemed most relevant to you and bookmark it. Keep yourself and your child familiar with the methods that are needed to maintain good school attendance. Practice will not necessarily make perfect attendance, but good practice will help prevent serious problems from developing in the future.

Continue to keep track of your child's distress, morning behaviors, and attendance every day. I know it may be tempting to stop completing the worksheets, especially because of the busy lives we lead. However, children who once had trouble going to school sometimes have additional trouble going to school later on. One way to reduce the chance of this happening is to constantly track your child's behavior. If your child knows that you are tracking him, then he will be less likely to miss school. Always know where your child is and, when necessary, have him complete a daily attendance log even when he is back to school full time (see Chapter 6). In addition, you may wish to have someone at school help monitor your child during the day and let you know if attendance problems occurred or nearly occurred.

Remain in close contact with relevant school officials throughout the school year. As I have mentioned several times in this book, a good working relationship with school officials is essential for returning a child to school and for preventing problems in the future. Continue to work with school officials so they can let you know immediately if your child has left school. School officials can also keep you informed about other problems that might lead to school absences. Examples include mood changes, social isolation, incomplete schoolwork, and disruptive behavior, among others. In addition, let school officials know immediately if *you* are having new problems getting your child to school. That way, a plan can be developed to address problems quickly before they get worse.

Meet with school officials if you suspect that threats or school climate issues may lead to future attendance problems. Examples of threats include bullies or others who intimidate or terrorize students. Examples of school climate issues include poor teacher attitudes, inappropriate curricula, oppressive environments for diverse students, and difficult learning situations. If your child complains of these kinds of problems, then meet with school officials to seek solutions before school attendance becomes too difficult.

Meet with your child for at least 10 minutes each evening to review the day at school. Do not let things pile up or get bottled up. Let your child vent about his school day, try to help him solve problems that might lead to future absences, help him practice the methods described in this book, and be supportive. If your child knows that you are willing to carve out some private time to discuss school issues, then he will probably be more willing to work with you to help solve problems that arise. If legitimate problems do arise, then discuss these issues with school officials as soon as possible. Do not allow obstacles to school attendance to grow. Also, talk to your child about times he was most tempted to leave school and how he handled this situation.

Practice the methods in this book during breaks from school. Even during holiday breaks and summertime, make sure your child practices relaxation methods, socializes with other kids, stays on a regular morning routine, and gets enough sleep. Do your part also. Even during breaks, give appropriate rewards and disincentives and good commands and always know where your child is and who he is spending time with. The more you use these methods, the more they become automatic or "second nature," which will help prevent future school attendance problems.

Remind your child of the success he had going back to school. Occasionally tell your child how proud you are that he went back to school. *Never take your child's school attendance for granted!* You may want to take pictures of accomplishments your child made when going back to school. Examples include riding the school bus alone, entering the school building without your help, speaking to other kids at school, giving an oral presentation, and performing at a concert. These are significant accomplishments, so praise your child for them! In addition, praise your child for continuing to do difficult things like going to school each day.

Continue to ignore minor complaints about having to attend school. Your child may "test" you later on by complaining about school, crying about being away from you, or feeling unwell. Be supportive but do not give these behaviors and statements too much attention. Again, let your rewards, disincentives, and agreements do your talking for you. And do not worry too much if your child does start complaining again about school. Some parents think, "Here we go again!" and assume they are back to "square one." But this is not the case. Your child is likely seeing what kind of reaction he can get from you. If your child sees that he is not going to get away with anything, that he has to go to school and that you are not falling into this trap, then his complaints will taper off.

Expect your child to attend school every day. This is more an attitude than anything else, but the idea is that you should expect attendance rather than absence from school. *Every day!* Adopting this attitude frees you from worry about what will happen in the morning because *only extraordinary events* (hazardous weather, severe illness) should keep your child home from school. Make every effort to get your child to school even under challenging circumstances. Remember that it is far better for your child to go to school for 4 out of 6 hours than to miss school altogether. Always aim for at least some school attendance on any given day if possible. *Finally, no backsliding!* Once your child has shown that he can attend school and classes regularly, this is the *minimum behavior* you should expect.

Special Circumstances Regarding Your Family or Your Child

Your family or your child may have special circumstances that may limit the usefulness of the methods discussed in this book. One special circumstance is that you may have to leave for work before your child has to go to school. In this situation, have another adult stay with your child and ensure that he makes it to school. If no one is available, then arrange a supervised ride for your child to get to school. Be sure to check that he actually went to school and what went wrong if he did not. If the school attendance problem continues and you have no one else to take your child to school, then you may need to make special work arrangements so that you can go in later after you take your child to school. Work with school officials re-garding possible transportation options as well.

Another special circumstance involves multiple children in a family who are having difficulty attending school. You may have two or three children of different ages with trouble attending school. Or you may have one child who is refusing to go to school and another child who is starting to copy behaviors such as dawdling or tantrums. If your children have difficulty attending school for the same reason, such as to get attention from you, then you can use the methods described in this book for each child (see Chapter 5). If your children have difficulty attending school for different reasons, then you could use different methods for each child (such as Chapter 3 for one child and Chapter 5 for another child). Or you could use both methods for both children. Both children could practice relaxation exercises (see Chapter 3), and both could be on a set morning schedule with rewards and disincentives (see Chapter 5).

Another option is to spend most of your time working with the child who is missing the most school or has the most difficult school attendance problems. In this case, use the methods in this book and concentrate most on this child. As the other children see what is happening, which we hope involves more school attendance, they may be more likely to go to school themselves. Finally, and most importantly in this situation, *get help!* Find other people who can help you complete the morning routine and help take your kids to school.

Another special circumstance involves children with developmental disorders who have difficulty attending school. This may include a child with a learning disorder who is frustrated about his schoolwork but may also include children with severe developmental disorders such as autism or intellectual disability. In these cases, work closely with school officials to design an accommodation plan (Chapter 6) that includes methods to improve school attendance such as the ones described in this book. This is especially important for designing part-time attendance schedules. In addition, meet with school officials often to see what problems at school might be resolved. If a child with a reading disorder feels unmotivated, then extra tutoring and a reward-based program at school might be helpful.

Another special circumstance involves families who have been referred to the legal/court system because of their child's absenteeism. School officials will sometimes refer a family to the legal/court system should a child miss a lot of school. If this has happened, then get as much information as you can about what is going to happen next. Do you need a lawyer? Do you have to meet with a juvenile detention officer? Do you have to go to "truancy" court?

Every state is different, so I cannot give you detailed recommendations about what will happen. My general recommendation is to work closely with school and legal officials to resolve your child's school attendance problems as soon as possible. Show that you are motivated to help solve this problem by attending meetings and doing what you can to get your child in school for at least part of the day. School and legal officials are generally more interested in getting a child back to school than in pursuing formal charges.

What to Do If This Book Was Less Helpful

I hope you found the methods in this book to be helpful, but what if problems seem to be lingering? Some parents say that their child now goes to school for part of the day but cannot seem to go a full day. Other parents say their child now goes to school but still seems upset. Other parents say that nothing worked. What now?

A couple of things might be happening. *First*, perhaps the methods in this book have not yet been tried long enough. I know it takes a lot of patience and persistence, but school attendance problems sometimes need to be worked on for at least a few weeks before significant results are seen. In addition, the longer a child has been having problems going to school, the longer it usually takes for him to go back to school. If a school attendance problem has been developing for some time, it will take some time to fix. If you have been using the methods for only a couple of weeks, then I encourage you to keep going. Meet with school officials to set up a timeline for these methods. You and they may agree to try certain methods for 3 weeks and then evaluate whether they are working. If not, then the methods could be "tweaked" a bit or a new strategy could be tried.

Second, perhaps the methods in this book are not being used consistently. Because a child's school attendance problems can be unpredictable, parents sometimes use the methods in this book on "bad" days and not on "good" days. Many parents wait and see what kind of behavior they are going to get from their child in the morning and then *respond* to the behavior ("dancing to the child's tune"; see

Chapter 5). A child may dawdle one morning, so parents use the structured morning routine. On another day, he may get ready for school with little problem, so the structured morning routine is given less thought.

Being inconsistent holds several dangers. One danger is that you are constantly responding to your child's behavior instead of the other way around. Your child must respond to *your* expectations, rules, rewards, disincentives, and meetings. If you consistently use a set morning routine or an agreement, then your child is always responding to what *you* set up and not the other way around. Another danger of being inconsistent is that children will not take seriously the methods described in this book. They are looking to you as the role model, so if you do not take the methods seriously, they also will not. Finally, being inconsistent allows children to think they might be able to exploit the situation and miss school. Children are more willing to test their parents if they know that parents may "give in" and allow them to miss school.

Third, perhaps some other problem is going on that prevents the methods in this book from being fully effective. Something unusual may have happened while you were trying to get your child to go back to school: the birth of a new baby, an illness in the family, a car accident, job loss, a sudden move to a new area, or some other special event that may have caused distress. If this is the case, then think about whether you can truly put forth the effort needed to get your child back in school with less distress. If you feel you can, then see how you can "work around" major events to still accomplish what you want to accomplish. If Mom is in the hospital, can other people help bring a child to school?

If you do not feel truly able to get your child back in school at this time, then work closely with school officials to let them know what is happening. Schedule an extended timeline for getting your child back to school or seek a "stopgap" measure such as an alternative school format so your child is receiving an education while you are managing other stressors (see also Chapter 8). Try not to delay your child's education if possible.

Fourth, this book may not be completely right for your situation. In Chapter 1 and in other chapters, I outlined different situations that might make this book less helpful. Examples include school attendance problems for a long period of time, severe behavior problems in addition to school attendance problems, and intense conflict among family members. If you find that you cannot use the methods in this book because of these or other situations, then you may wish to consult a qualified mental health professional (see Chapter 1). A qualified mental health professional can help you address more intense problems that you may be facing. In many cases, school attendance problems are simply one part of these intense problems. A qualified mental health professional can help you handle all of these problems because he or she will know the unique issues that you are facing. Chapter 8 also covers additional suggestions for severe school attendance problems.

8

Severe School Attendance Problems and Extended Time Out of School

Alejandro is a 16-year-old boy who has been out of school for much of the past 2 years. He began to disengage from school in eighth grade and especially from his core classes in math, English, and science. Alejandro started to skip classes and miss entire days in middle school, and his school attendance problems became much worse in high school. He has passed only three courses in 2 years of high school and is already far behind with respect to credits earned toward graduation. Alejandro says he often feels isolated at school because he does not understand much of what is happening in his classes and no longer has close friends or social contacts at school. His school counselor has indicated that Alejandro is at high risk of not meeting requirements for graduation.

This book is designed mostly to help parents solve school attendance problems that have lasted less than 4 months or that are less severe in nature. Many school attendance problems like Alejandro's, however, last more than 4 months and often much longer. These *severe* kinds of school attendance problems are often marked by sporadic or little attendance and sometimes legal problems as a result. Severe school attendance problems can also involve serious emotional and behavioral difficulties, such as intense anxiety, depression, disruptiveness, aggression, and substance use. Many students with severe attendance problems like Alejandro fall far behind in their course material, fail multiple classes or have poor grades, and gain few credits toward graduation. Social problems can occur as well, such as disconnection from classmates and withdrawal from school activities. Teenagers with severe school attendance problems are at increased risk for dropping out of school.

In previous chapters, I covered ways to solve less severe school attendance problems. In this chapter, I discuss:

- Possible avenues forward for youth with severe attendance problems
- Suggestions for dealing with extended periods of time out of school

Severe School Attendance Problems

Teenagers with severe school attendance problems like Alejandro often start to become disengaged during their middle school years and then gradually miss more classes during their high school years. Unfortunately, high school is the time when grades count the most and when formal credits are gained toward graduation. Once a teenager falls so far behind in courses and credits, the path toward finishing high school and graduation becomes less clear. He or she is at risk for dropping out of school.

In most cases of severe school attendance problems, a return to full-time school attendance in a regular classroom setting is a challenging and daunting task. Most teenagers in this situation are very disconnected from their classes and peers and have no desire to return to a traditional school setting. These teenagers may also have intense anxiety or depression that prevents them from being able to return to a regular classroom setting. Many families in this situation also feel helpless and hopeless and are confused about what to do next.

If your teenager has severe school attendance problems, then consider two main courses of action moving forward. *One course of action* is to work with school officials on a nontraditional, alternative path toward graduation. This alternative path could include different learning formats, such as virtual or online learning or a hybrid approach that involves some online learning and in-person instruction. Another alternative path could include modified credit requirements toward graduation or different ways in which those credits could be gained. Instead of in-class instruction, for example, other methods to gain credits, such as portfolios, could be used (see section below).

Another course of action is to work with professionals at your child's school and in the community who can help with other, related problems that may have arisen with the school attendance problems. Related problems might include academic difficulties, emotional and behavioral issues, and family conflict, among others. Families often need help managing not only complicated school-related issues but also mental health and other concerns that seem overwhelming. Let's talk about these two courses of action in the next sections.

Alternative Paths to Graduation

Many school districts have alternative schools or academic programs to help teenagers with severe school attendance problems graduate from high school. Your first task will be to *schedule a meeting with your child's school counselor or other administrator* to talk about what alternative options are available in your school district and which of these options might be best for your child. You will want to talk about your child's current academic status (grades, credits gained toward graduation); how your child might be able to graduate on time or slightly later; and what flexibility different alternative options have that might be a good fit for your situation and your child's interest.

Develop a plan that is most workable for your family and your current circumstances. This may mean developing a formal accommodation plan (Chapter 6) for your child. Think about whether your child is willing and able to try the new plan, what transportation and academic supplies might be needed, whether the new schedule is realistic, and how the plan matches up with mental health and other services your family may be receiving (next section). A brief description of alternative options is presented next but remember that each school district has different options available.

Alternative options include afterschool opportunities that may involve tutoring, classes during the evening or weekends, community service, and medical and mental health services. Other alternative options allow credits to be gained in nontraditional ways, such as through special examinations, portfolios (collection of finished works or projects), modular (briefer) courses, and online instruction. Home-based programs may be available as well and can include visiting teachers, parent-led instruction, or hybrid instruction that combines home, distance, and in-school learning. Some school districts also offer seniors an extra fifth year, perhaps combined with summer work, to help students graduate on time or close to on time.

Some school districts have separate school buildings that center more on specialized academic areas such as science and technology. Alternative school options sometimes focus on experiential learning, or hands-on learning or learning through experience on a certain skill or project. They may also concentrate on helping students reach appropriate grade level with respect to core areas such as reading, math, and science. These schools are sometimes linked to dominant businesses in a given area, such as agriculture, tourism, or different types of engineering.

Some school districts partner with community colleges or other community agencies to help teenagers graduate from high school and prepare for their next step in adulthood at the same time. This might involve some academic work combined with community service and occupational or vocational training in a certain job skill. Social service and mental health support are sometimes part of these programs as well. In addition, residential schools are sometimes available for teenagers who have been involved with the court system but who also receive educational and mental health services.

Again, speak with school officials about which alternative path to graduation might be best for your child. Be sure to discuss any obstacles to this path that might need to be addressed before the plan is put in place. Meet regularly with school officials to talk about how the plan is progressing and whether changes are needed. Talk to your teenager as well about how he or she is adjusting to the new schedule and whether additional support is needed. In addition, try to link this academic plan with community support, which is discussed next.

Community Support

Your child and family may need added support beyond the educational process. As mentioned, many families with a child with severe school attendance problems struggle with mental health issues and family conflict. In Chapter 1, I talked about the possible need to consult with a clinical child psychologist or psychiatrist who can help with mental health problems. Other resources include social workers, family therapists, counselors, and other licensed professionals. Talk to school officials or local mental health agencies about who might be best for your situation.

Find a therapist who can help you and your family manage mental health and other problems and who can work with school officials to help solve severe school attendance problems. Sometimes a teenager with intense anxiety or depression will need therapy *before* trying a new school experience or will need help as he enters a new academic program. Many kids who have been out of school for a long time also need to relearn new skills. Therapists can work with teachers and other school officials to develop accommodation plans and to help develop academic skills like studying and time management, social skills like starting conversations or performing before others, and life skills such as critical thinking and self-control. Therapists can also work with families to ease conflict, improve communication, and problem-solve more effectively.

Extensive Time Out of School

Education is undergoing many changes. Some of these changes are internal to a school district, such as greater focus on distance or online learning. Other changes are external to a school district and involve factors beyond its control that lead to extended periods of time when kids are home from school. Crises such as pandemics, natural disasters, or episodes of violence can cause school districts to shut down periodically or for lengthy periods of time. This forces parents and children to adjust to an uneven school schedule and learning process. Suggestions for navigating these unsettling periods of time are presented next.

If your child is out of school for an extended period of time due to a school closure, then *maintaining a regular but flexible daily routine or schedule* is very important. In Chapter 5, I outlined in detail what a *morning* school preparation routine might look like. If a child is to be learning at home during a school shutdown, then the morning routine should proceed as if the child were going to school on a regular day. In addition, setting a routine for the "school" day at home after the morning routine is completed is important. Sometimes, this "day" routine is set by a school district with live, distance-based classes, but other times children are expected to do more independent work.

Schedule a daily routine that is *flexible and reasonable* for your child's age and attention span (many examples are available online). Kids often struggle to stay motivated learning at home, so you want to avoid overloading them with too much academic work. Instead, set times for different academic subjects and mix these times with creative projects, exercise, and lunch and other breaks. Creative projects can also include learning different life skills like how to cook spaghetti, work the washing machine, or tend a garden. In this way, tasks around the home are completed and the child is learning at the same time. Reward your child for completing academic work and these other kinds of projects.

The daily routine should also involve limiting access to electronic devices unless they are needed for academic lessons. Focus more on having your child read *each day*. Try to find a place in your home that is more for schoolwork and studying and less for fun electronic devices. As much as possible, stick to schoolwork and other tasks during "school" hours and dinner and other activities during "nonschool" or evening hours. Doing so will also help ease the process back to regular school once the shutdown ends.

Many schools in a shutdown still offer academic services, meals, and opportunities to connect with others using appropriate social distancing. Take advantage of these opportunities. Students in particular should maintain close contacts with their teachers and ask questions about current topics, assignments, course expectations, makeup work, and other areas. Parents can also interact with teachers to learn new skills, such as factoring polynomials or balancing chemical equations. Interacting with teachers also provides an extra social contact that is helpful during shutdown periods. Many online resources are also available for parents and children learning on their own.

Talk to your kids during the shutdown about any emotional reactions they may be having, such as loneliness or worry about school starting again or being away from friends. Try to have them connect with friends as much as possible in a safe environment. If extracurricular activities are available, then encourage your child to participate in them or spend time outdoors. Limit the news as needed. Help your child manage distress (Chapters 3 and 4), get enough sleep, eat properly, and take steps to stay physically healthy, like regularly washing hands.

When children do go back to school, try to adjust to the new routine but understand that this may take some time. Talk to teachers and other school officials about how they plan to ease children back into the academic process and to work through emotional and other issues that resulted from the school shutdown. Encourage your child to reconnect with her classmates and other peers to rebuild social relationships. Continue to talk to your child about any emotional reactions he is having because of the changes in circumstances.

School closures and shutdowns for any reason can be stressful on everyone. Understand that everyone in the home will need to stay flexible and patient as adjustments are made. Be kind to one another. Remember that all you can do is your best, and that you are just trying to maintain basic skills until school reopens. If this means just focusing on reading and a few math problems, that is fine. Keep your expectations realistic and feel free to change the daily process as circumstances change or as people in the home change. Hang in there!

Additional Resources

All of the methods described in this book are based on scientific research and my extensive experience working with kids with school attendance problems. Although it is not necessary to read the technical information behind the methods covered in this book, some people like to read additional material to find out more about the nature, cause, assessment, and treatment of school attendance problems in children. An "Additional Resources" section at the back of this book contains a list of books and journal articles that contain further information on school attendance problems.

Final Comments

Thank you for reading this book! I appreciate the fact that you are willing to make the effort to get your child back to school with less distress. I hope you find my recommendations helpful now and in the future. If you find that your child's school attendance problems have some special circumstance that I did not cover in this book, please let me know. Most of all, remember that you are not alone. Many parents face what you are facing, and many professionals study this problem. Together we can make a difference!

Additional Resources

Kearney, C. A. (2016). *Managing school absenteeism at multiple tiers: An evidence-based and practical guide for professionals.* Oxford University Press.

Kearney, C. A. (2018). *Helping school refusing children and their parents: A guide for school-based professionals* (2nd ed.). Oxford University Press.

Kearney, C. A. (2019). *Helping families of youth with school attendance problems: A practical guide for mental health and school-based professionals.* Oxford University Press.

Kearney, C. A., & Albano, A. M. (2018). *When children refuse school: A cognitive-behavioral therapy approach/parent workbook* (3rd ed.). Oxford University Press.

Kearney, C. A., Gonzálvez, C., Graczyk, P. A., & Fornander, M. (2019a). Reconciling contemporary approaches to school attendance and school absenteeism: Toward promotion and nimble response, global policy review and implementation, and future adaptability (Part 1). *Frontiers in Psychology, 10,* 2222. https://doi.org/10.3389/fpsyg.2019.02222

Kearney, C. A., Gonzálvez, C., Graczyk, P. A., & Fornander, M. (2019b). Reconciling contemporary approaches to school attendance and school absenteeism: Toward promotion and nimble response, global policy review and implementation, and future adaptability (Part 2). *Frontiers in Psychology, 10,* 2605. https://dx.doi.org/10.3389%2Ffpsyg.2019.02605

Kearney, C. A., & Graczyk, P. A. (2020). A multidimensional, multi-tiered system of supports model to promote school attendance and address school absenteeism. *Clinical Child and Family Psychology Review, 23*(3), 316–337. https://doi.org/10.1007/s10567-020-00317-1

Ollendick, T. H., & Cerny, J. A. (1981). *Clinical behavior therapy with children.* Springer.

Silverman, W. K., & Kurtines, W. M. (1996). *Anxiety and phobic disorders: A pragmatic approach.* Springer.

Index

Tables and figures are indicated by *t* and *f* following the page number.